The Shock of Arrival

Reflections on Postcolonial Experience

By Meena Alexander

South End Press Boston, MA

Text design and production by South End Press collective
Printed in the U.S.A.

Library of Congress Cataloging-in-Publication Data

Alexander, Meena
The shock of arrival: reflections on Postcolonial experience/
by Meena Alexander.
   p.   cm.
   ISBN 0-89608-546-5 (cloth). —ISBN 0-89608-545-7 (paper)
   1. East Indian Americans—Ethnic identity. 2. East Indian
Americans—Language. 3. Women immigrants—United States.
4. United States—Ethnic relations. 5. Imperialism—Psychological
aspects.
   I. Title
   E184.E2A44   1996
   305.891'4073—dc20
                        96-15058
                        CIP

02 01 00 99 98 97 96   1 2 3 4 5 6 7 8

® GCIU 745-C

Contents

Author's Note

My thanks to Alastair Niven and the Arts Council for an invitation to visit England as an International Writer in Residence. And to friends with whom I shared thoughts while working on this project: Talal Asad, Erika Duncan, Sara Suleri Goodyear, Inderpal Grewal, May Joseph, Walter Kendrick, Nalini Natarajan, Roshni Rustomji, Susan Sherman, Ella Shohat, Amritjit Singh, Neil Tolchin, Gauri Viswanathan. Their insights have helped me on. My thanks to David Lelyveld and our children Adam and Svati for their patience and understanding. My special gratitude to Sonia Shah for her belief in this book and the care with which she guided me through.

'I am very curious. Tell me everything about yourself starting with your birth. Where were you born? Who gave you your name? ... Do you remember what happened to you in another life?... How were you caught in this cage?'

—The king to the suka bird
Banabhatta, *Kadambari*

Another Voice

'From the eyesight proceeds another eyesight and from the hearing proceeds another hearing and from the voice proceeds another voice...'

—Walt Whitman, *Leaves of Grass*

The poems and prose pieces in this book braid together difficult truths of body and language. Though they rise out of various moments in my life, each was created under the sign of America. Migrancy, a central theme for many of us in this shifting world, forces a recasting of how the body is grasped, how language works. Then, too, at the heart of what happens in these sometimes jagged reflections of mine, is the question of postcolonial memory.

The shock of arrival is multifold—what was borne in the mind is jarred, tossed into new shapes, an exciting exfoliation of sense. What we were in that other life, is shattered open. But the worlds we now inhabit still speak of the need for invention, of ancestors, of faith. In a time of literally explosive possibilities, we must figure out how to live our lives.

The shock of arrival forces us to new knowledge. What the immigrant must work with is what she must invent in order to live. Race, ethnicity, the fluid truths of gender are all cast afresh. Nationality, too, that emptiest and yet most contested of signs, marks us.

The old question 'Who am I?' returns—I am what others see me as, but I am also my longings, my desire, my speech. But how is that speech formed, when what they see me as cuts against the grain of what I sense myself to be? Coming to America, I have felt in my own heart what W.E.B. Dubois invoked: 'two souls, two thoughts…in one dark body.'

But now, at the tail end of the century, perhaps there are many souls, many voices in one dark body.

And how does this consciousness work, here, now, for an Indian woman?

What multifoliate truth is stirring here?

What buried voices, quickening?

Piecemeal Shelters

The act of writing, it seems to me, makes up a shelter, allows space to what would otherwise be hidden, crossed out, mutilated. Sometimes writing can work toward a reparation, making a sheltering space for the mind. Yet it feeds off ruptures, tears in what might otherwise seem a seamless, oppressive fabric. Surely this difficult sense of how the writing life works was caused, in part, by growing up female in a traditional Indian home. While it was fine to read and write, the writing that came out of image and desire—and what else might a poem be?—was dangerous, filled with disclosures that could split the fine skin of decorum, threaten hierarchy, the accustomed flow of household, even public order. But to a young girl in a Syrian Christian household, raised both in Kerala and in North Africa, grand distinctions between public and private spaces had little relevance, no more relevance than they had for her in writing poems where it was essential that the imagination create an intense, if necessarily brief, fusion of disparate worlds, fracturing thoughts.

Since these acts of writing are framed by a world, itself more or less governed by the strictures of colonialism, the impulse to write touches off an almost wordless excess in the self. And attempts to gain access to an intimate language that can also work in the public sphere—essential for an imaginative writer— can turn harsh, even bruising. The truths of self, far from being sanctioned by tradition, ratified by a body of canonical knowledge, seem mere eruptions, one-shot affairs, nervous outbursts of desire.

I was born a few years after Indian independence and learned English both in India and in North Africa. The English I learned in India was always braided in with other languages: Hindi, for I was born in Allahabad and spent my earliest years there; Malayalam, the language of my parents; Tamil, which was spoken by friends; Marathi, for I spent a year in Pune. In contrast, the English I learnt from a Scottish tutor in Khartoum and then perfected in the Diocesan School for British children was strict, and given the sternness of colonial pedagogy, cut away from the Arabic that flowed all around, from French, and from my mother tongue Malayalam, even from the sort of English I spoke with my parents and friends.

It was as if a white skin had covered over that language of accomplishment and I had to pierce through it, tear it open in order to make it supple, fluid enough to accomodate the murmurings of my own heart.

This process of tearing away, of stripping the language of its canonical burden, of its colonial consolations—by which I also mean the haunting elegiac mask of the Wordsworthian paradigm—is hard indeed. And there were years when I felt I need not dirty my hands with the task of facing up to the violence implicit in the very language I used: English. Surely the impulses of feeling and of thought, surely the lyric voice in whatever intensity it could muster was enough, enough resistance. And if there was tumult in the streets, gunshots, rape, the elegaic voice might still persist.

It was a shock to me, a crisis in my writing life, if not in all the rest of what goes on under that phrase—my life, as if it were an elixir I possessed and might drink to the full or spit out as I chose—to realise that the machine of the colonial, technically postcolonial education I had received and, indeed, had fostered, was cutting my words off from the very wellsprings of desire. Suddenly, I felt that even memory would be impossible if I did not turn my attention to the violence very close at hand, attendant, in fact, upon the procedures of my own writing.

This awareness fused with the need to voice the truths of the female body, precisely that which had been torn away, cast out from the linguistic awareness I had refined. I searched around for ways to go. I read Toru Dutt, Sarojini Naidu, the fierce tumultuous works of Lalithambika Antherjanam, who, writing in Malayalam from a Namboodiri household, was able to tear apart the skin of decorum, of the ritually prescribed feminine, precisely all that marked as polluted and polluting, the fierce desires of her female figures. Sarojini Naidu, however, for all her growing political involvement with Mohandas Gandhi in the years before Indian independence, was never able to cut free of the poetic ideology, the tight stanzas of pale, figurative constraint she had picked up from Arthur Symons and Gosse in her studies in England.

I read others, contemporary writers: Audre Lorde, Toni Morrison, Gloria Anzaldua, Leslie Marmon Silko from the United States; Michelle Cliff, Edward Brathwaite, Edouard Glissant from the Caribbean; Tayib Salih from Sudan; Aliffa Riffat and Nawal el Sadaawi from Egypt; Assia Djebar from Algeria; Tahar Ben Jelloun from Morocco; Wole Soyinka from Nigeria; Ngugi wa Thiong'o from Kenya. In his book, *Decolonising the Mind*, Ngugi wa Thiong'o reveals the grim truth about the violence implicit in his study of English: the forced repetitions, the beatings, the deliberate shaming of those who dared to speak in Gikuyu, all components of a cultural complex underwritten by the imperial need to maintain territorial power. And while I had never borne any of that literal physical punishment, the psychological scars of how I came to English are still vivid. They have stayed with me in my writing life.

And so the questions of colonialism bleed into an era of decolonization, into the complicated realms of American ethnicity. They mark our memory. Our spiritual flesh cannot be torn apart, cannot be cleansed. I think of the haunting lines in Theresa Cha's *Dictée*. The image is that of a fine cloth folded, perhaps a handkerchief: 'Already there are folds remnant from the previous foldings now leaving a permanent mark.' Elsewhere in the same book, she writes of how the stain begins to absorb the material it is spilt on.

Memory in this postcolonial world transforms what lies around it. The present moves to jagged rhythms, the brusque and hidden laws of our dislocation. What I recollect best is what shines up in the face of present danger, luminous with the shock of arrival. All that I see and touch in this arena of our displacement is to be elaborated, spelled out, precariously reconstructed.

But what of the imperial quarters that were left behind by those who thought they could capture our earlier world? Those colonial structures are torn down and burning. In my novel *Nampally Road*, inside a burning police station in Hyderabad, built long ago by the British, the narrator puts out her hand and touches the cheek of Rameeza Be, the woman who had been gang-raped by the police.

'See, they meet in the cell, in the police station the people will set on fire. This is where they first meet,' a young woman who was reading the book pointed out to me. 'Did you know that?'

'No,' I replied, 'I had never thought it out to myself in that way, but now that you say it, I see.'

She persisted: 'Why do they meet there?'

And though I was curiously inarticulate when I faced her, I now try to answer as best I can: because of the oppression the narrator must face, the violence that has consumed the life of another woman. And now I think: where but in the burning police station, facing the cell bars, should the narrator herself, dislocated, displaced, face up to things as they are?

At the end of the novel, in a riot scene, the walls of the old house are torn down. But the woman who was raped has entered the house and faces the narrator. If I were to write an aftermath to that novel, I would speak of how eventually they go out into the streets together, for our histories are lived out in public places. And these places gather sense through language.

For a writer of the South Asian diaspora, the habitations that language might provide—whatever the language, Hindi, Marathi, Gujarathi, English—are always conjured up, imaginary shelters that can only be piecemeal. The writer is haunted by the radical nature of dislocation, not singular, but multiple, given the world as it comes to us now—not just in the dailiness of our lives, waking up, walking down a winter street, setting down 50¢ for a newspaper, but in the manifold figurations of knowledge, through CNN, faxes, E-mail, the visible buying and selling of multinational corporations, the invisible telephone lines that link New York with Delhi or Tiruvella and, with their rough oceanic sounds, threaten to obliterate beloved voices.

Then, too, walking down a crowded sidewalk, descending the subway, there is always one's own body, which is marked as Other in this country. Ethnicity can draw violence. And this is part of the postcolonial terrain, part of the sorrow and knowledge of our senses.

To make space for what was crossed out in the decorum of femininity, in the high places of a classical hierarchy, in the racism of a canonical knowledge, in the obliterations of a national memory—where the terrors of repeated bombardment are left behind with yesterday's best seller list—all this is part of our task, part of the violent, fractured worlds that we must etch into beauty.

And so the shelters the mind makes up are crisscrossed by borders, weighted down as a tent might be by multiple anchorages, ethnic solidarities, unselvings.

'They refused to sell me gas, the man yelled at me, he said I was an Iraqi, that they would kill us all,' my friend Zarina told me, recounting her experiences on Ninth Avenue this spring. 'Who are we, Meena?' she continued. 'Where are we? Where are our lives?' I was silent as she spoke. I stood on the sidewalk next to her, staring at a patch of blue sky in between two skyscrapers.

Now, I want to turn to her and say: we are here in this present, the only one we have, fractured, pitted, pitched to violence. Under the pressure of our present, fault lines in our earth fill with remembered fragrances, a lost petal, torn mango leaf, dried blood on a young child's sleeve.

Art of Pariahs

Back against the kitchen stove
Draupadi sings:

In my head Beirut still burns.*

The Queen of Nubia, of God's Upper Kingdom,
the Rani of Jhansi, transfigured, raising her sword,
are players too. They have entered with me
into North America and share these walls.

We make up an art of pariahs:

Two black children spray painted white,
their eyes burning,
a white child raped in a car
for her pale skin's sake,
an Indian child stoned by a bus shelter,
they thought her white in twilight.

Someone is knocking and knocking
but Draupadi will not let him in.
She squats by the stove and sings:

The Rani shall not sheathe her sword

---

* Note: The line 'Beirut still burns' is something I saw written on a wall in the East
Village. The poem itself, "Art of Pariahs," was occasioned by a series of racist
incidents that took place in New York City. I imagine Draupadi of the
Mahabharata, become a young Indian woman in North America.

nor Nubia's queen restrain her elephants
till tongues of fire wrap a tender blue,
a second skin, a solace to our children.

Come walk with me toward a broken wall
—Beirut still burns—carved into its face.
Outcastes all, let's conjure honey scraped from stones,
an underground railroad stacked with rainbow skin,
Manhattan's mixed rivers rising.

Language and Shame

There is something molten in me. I do not know how else to begin, all over again as if in each attempt something needs to be recast, rekindled, some bond, some compact between flesh, clothing, words. There is something incendiary in me and it has to do with being female, here, now, in America. And those words, those markers, of gender, of time, of site, all have an extraordinary valency. When they brush up against each other, each of those markers—'female,' 'here,' 'now,' 'America'—I find that there is something quite unstable in the atmosphere they set up. I do not have a steady, taken for granted compact with my body. Nor indeed with my language. Yet it is only as my body enters into, coasts through, lives in language that I can make sense.

I need to go backwards, to begin: think of language and shame.

As a child I used to hide out to write. This was in Khartoum, where I spent many months of each year—my life divided between that desert land and the tropical green of Kerala, where my mother returned with her children for the summer months. In Khartoum, I hid behind the house under a neem tree or by a cool wall. Sometimes I forced myself into the only room where I could close the door, the toilet. I gradually learnt that the toilet was safer, no one would thrust the door open on me. There I could mind my own business and compose. I also learnt to write in snatches. If someone knocked at the door, I stopped abruptly, hid my papers under my skirts, tucked my pen into the elastic band of my knickers, and got up anxiously. Gradually, this enforced privacy—for I absorbed and perhaps, in part, even identified with my mother's disapproval over my poetic efforts—added an aura of something illicit, shameful, to my early sense of my scribblings. Schoolwork was seen in a totally different light. It was good to excel there, interpreting works that were part of a great literary past. The other writing, in one's own present, was to be tucked away, hidden. No wonder then that my entry into the realm of letters was fraught.

The facts of multilingualism added complexity to this split sense of writing in English. Hindi washed over me in my earliest years. I chattered aloud in it to the children around. It was my first spoken language, though Malayalam, my mother tongue, has always been there by its side, indeed alongside any other language I have used. What is my mother tongue now, if not a buried stream? At times, in America, I feel my mother tongue approaches the condition of dream. Its curving syllables blossom for me in so many scripts: gawky, dazzling letters spray painted in fluorescent shades onto the metal sides of subway cars or the dark walls of inner tunnels, shifting, metamorphic. Sometimes in chalk I read letters a man draws out laboriously on the sidewalks of Manhattan, spelling out the obvious, as necessity so often compels: I AM HOMELESS, I NEED FOOD, SHELTER. A smattering of dimes and quarters lie near his bent knees. Those letters I read in the only script I know make for a ferocious, almost consumptive edge to knowledge in me.

I have never learnt to read or write in Malayalam and turned into a truly postcolonial creature, who had to live in English, though a special sort of English, I must say, for the version of the language I am comfortable with bends and sways to the shores of other territories, other tongues.

Yet the price of fluency in many places may well be loss of the sheer intimacy that one has with 'one's own' culture, a speech that holds its own sway, untouched by any other. But perhaps there is a dangerous simplicity here. And, indeed, how might such an idealized state be maintained at the tail end of the century? And it is a dangerous idea that animates such simplicity, small and bloody wars have been fought for such ideals.

Of course, there are difficulties in the way of one who does not know how to read or write her mother tongue. For instance, I would love to read the prose of Lalithambika Antherjanam, the poetry of Nalapat Balamaniamma and Ayyappa Paniker rather than have them read to me. I would love to read Mahakavi K.V. Seemon's epic *Vedaviharam* rather than have it recited to me.

Or is there something in me that needs to draw on that old reliance, the voice of another reading, the sheer giveness of speech. After all, if it were just an issue of mother wit, I am sure I would be able to read and write Malayalam by now. So is there perhaps a deliberate dependency, revealing something of my childhood longings and fears, a community held in dream, a treasured orality? For the rhythms of the language first came to me not just in lullabies or in the chatter of women in the kitchen or by the wellside, but in the measured cadences of oratory and poetry, and nightly recitations from the Bible and the epics.

Perhaps there is a fear that learning the script would force me to face the tradition with its hierarchies, the exculsionary nature of canonical language. And how then would I be restored to simplicity, freed of the pressures of countermemory?

Sometimes all that has been forgotten wells up and I use my English to let it surface. At the end of "Night-Scene, the Garden," there is a vision of ancestors dancing free of the earth, permitting the 'ferocious alphabets of flesh.'

Alphabets of Flesh

My back against barbed wire
snagged and coiled to belly height
on granite posts
glittering to the moon

No man's land
no woman's either

I stand in the middle
of my life.

I cannot see my mother
I cannot see my father
I cannot see my sister
or my brother

Out of earth's soft
and turbulent core
a drum sounds
summoning ancestors

They rise
through puffs of greyish dirt
scabbed skins slit
and drop from them

They dance
atop the broken spurts
of stone

They scuff
the drum skins
with their flighty heels.

Men dressed
in immaculate white
bearing spears, and reams
of peeling leaf

Minute inscriptions
of our blood and race

Stumbling behind
in feverish coils
I watch the women come,
eyes averted from the threads
of smoke that spiral
from my face.

Some prise
their stiffening knuckles
from the iron grip
of pots and pans
and kitchen knives

Bolts of unbleached
cloth, embroidery needles,
glitter and crash in heaps.

. . . .

Slow accoutrements of habit
and of speech,
the lust of grief
the savagery of waste
flicker and burn
along the hedgerows
by the vine

The lost child
lifts her eyes to mine.

■ ■ ■ ■

Come ferocious alphabets of flesh
splinter and raze my page
That out of the dumb
and bleeding part of me
I may claim
my heritage.

The green tree
battened on despair
cast free

The green roots kindled
to cacophony.

■ ■ ■ ■

I had a lot of trouble writing that poem with the vision of the
'alphabets of flesh,' perhaps because of the muteness and illit-
eracy at the end, allowing me to identify with what is dumb and
bleeding.

It was around the same time that I wrote the poem "Passion," about the female experience of giving birth. The tenth

month, that limbo when one is no longer pregnant and not yet quite a mother. A condition I had read no poems about. I recall sitting on a mat, on the floor of a poet friend's house in Cuttack. I was reading the poem to Jayanta Mahapatra and his wife Runu. She asked me: 'But why the bird image? Where does it come from? How does it fit? It seems different, really.'

'I don't know. I think it was my way of conveying the intensity,' I replied. Now I think back, that's it: I wanted to convey something mute, unspeakable, brutal, everyday.

'Where do you write? When do you write?' someone asked me in Hyderabad after I gave a reading. My questioner, a political activist, was moved by "Passion" and had invited a Telugu writer to come and listen. He wanted to translate the poem into Telugu. 'I write in all kinds of places, including buses and subways,' I told her. 'Whenever and however I can.' That's the virtue of the miniature form of the poem—a word here, a line there, all sustained by the rhythm that beats in the head. I write on all kinds of paper, including kitchen towel.

I write on paper to reclaim ground. Even in Manhattan, where so little ground is visible. Marginality compels me to it, a territorial thing. And I ponder how these poems have come into being, how Manhattan, with its crowded streets and subways, frames the landscapes of my Indian imagination.

And somehow I say to myself, it has to be that way, the imagination claiming what was foreclosed. How else would I be able to touch where the shame is, tell it? How else could I feel the quick of a true desire? In living and writing here, as an Indian woman—even as in writing, in the intensity of that posture, there is a letting go, a burning up of the acts of accommodation that ordinary life works with—the self splits and multiplies, the dubiousness of one's estate, the shame even, turned into a thickness, a nourishment infolding the stuff of poetry, a torsion stylized, the quick step of marginality.

Passion

I.

After childbirth
the tenth month's passion:

a bloodiness
still shifting at her core
she crawls on the mud floor

past the empty rice sacks
blown large with dust,
rims distended like sails.

Her skin scrapes a tin bowl
with water from the stream,
a metal frame

bearing a god
whose black-blue face
melts into darkness, as a gem might

tossed back
into its own
implacable element.

She waits,
she sets her sari to her teeth
and when the chattering begins

fierce, inhuman joy,
monkeys rattling the jamun tree,
bellies distended, washed with wind

she screams
and screams
a raw, ungoverned thing.

II.

There are beetles scrabbling
in the open sacks,
chaff flies in the half-light
a savage sound in her eyes
struck free

the human realms of do and don't
the seemingly precise, unalterable keys
dashed to a frenzy
and still the voice holds.

III.

One summer's day
I saw a heron
small and grey
blinded by an eagle's claw

it dashed its head
against the Coromandel rock.

The bleeding head
hung on
by a sinew or two
as the maimed bird

struck
and struck again

then turned to rise
an instant
on its sunlit wings.

It was carved in bronze
against the crawling foam

agony
the dead cannot know
in their unaltered kingdoms.

IV.

I am she
the woman after giving birth

life
to give life
torn and hovering

as bloodied fluids
baste the weakened flesh.

For her
there are no words,
no bronze, no summoning.

I am her sight
her hearing
and her tongue.

I am she
smeared with ash
from the black god's altar

I am
the sting of love
the blood hot flute,
the face
carved in the window,
watching as the god set sail

across the waters
risen from the Cape,
Sri Krishna in a painted catamaran.

I am she
tongueless in rhapsody

the stars of glass
nailed to the Southern sky.

Ai ai

she cried.

They stuffed
her mouth with rags
and pulled her
from the wooden bed

and thrust her
to the broken floor.

I, I.

Skin Song

'Within the heart a mirror but no face shows
You'll see the face when the heart's doubleness goes.'

—Kabir

'Perceives that the corpse is slowly borne from the eating and
sleeping rooms of the house...'

— Whitman

I.

Time was a drift of wing, claw, vine,
petal, stalk, skin of my tongue, wrapping up
stones so sweet to suck. I skipped through dirt and muck
the short streams singing,
green scales dropped from my eyes
glittering in pieces.

I cannot spell it out
but when the hearse with black painted wheels
skirted the dirt, the bamboo grove hissed
the banana trees curtsied in heat, in terrible heat
I hid in a room.
On tiptoe I peered, throat between bars.

Water they had drawn for his last bath
sheened the mahogany.
Laid out naked his dear dark body
indigo globes of eyes, nostrils cast in bone,

feet arced, soles flecked with callouses.

II.

When the iron wheels on the hearse
cut into dirt and men dressed in white
sweat in their eyes strode by the wheels of the hearse
when the silvery groin of bamboo and lime
shimmered in dirt

Tongue thick with soil I roared, I belched my grief.
I was a catch in God's throat, a giggle, a gut gripe
I was vermilion threaded into rice paper
sheathe of sun and moon
time's masquerade

Slit in the vulva as the head
of the too-big-child tore the mother's tender skin.
I was speech swallowing death,
verbs all shame stanched: *Vak, Vak, Vak*
crouching, shitting, guts cramped in childbirth
the wide-shouldered bullheaded child
butting the mother-to-be.
She squats astride a blackness monstrous, driven deep
through lips that will not sleep.

'Amma Ila, amma,' whispers a girl child
licking a skein of dirt that drops from a mango tree.
It babbles on her tongue weave of silk, wood, dung
love's calumny.
She will not go to grandfather's funeral
watch his dear dark body shovelled into dirt.
Indoors she digs knuckles into eyes
rubs her face to the sky; does not cry.

III.

Now everything is hurt and harm
pebbles on a beach where water slops,
bold stripes on a child's skirt
a whip, a stripped cadence for a sun
that slits pink clouds to threads

She strolls on the beach
two children clinging to her
she sees very little,
by the water's edge over mounds of stone
waves flap, plastic shreds dance their rotting.
White sails are pasted to the horizon.

IV.

Time was a lyric did not sting
and a cloud cover over the kitchen wall
was streaked in gold,
but how grim it was under the crow's throat
the child stuffing herself with sweets
as rain slashed pillowcases,
delicate muslins in the windowsills.

In the kitchen under the rinsed blade
blood ran down the drain into the hill.

There was blood on her skirt
it was as her mother feared
it was not the juice of the black jamun
she rolled on her tongue, crushed in her gums
nor the overripe guava she spat at the sun
nor dribbled flesh of the watermelon.

With the pad between her legs
she could not walk very well
waddled at first, sidled as best she could
she learnt to wash out stains in cold water
with a bit of salt flung in.
She felt sore and shamed fresh and burnt.

Child of the soft mouth
the wordless part, remember me.

V.

Time was a python new killed
dripped its black stuff onto a dirt road
where the hearse stuck, wheels trapped in stones
elephants loitering in a temple processional
some hours earlier had loosed.

Time was the gap in the bars through which she peered
barefoot, square jawed.
She thrust her head toward the shower of light
from the gooseberry tree
glimpsed games marked on hands and knees

Grandfather and she playing at Ashoka's elephants
round and round the bed of tiger lilies
or peering through a bush, one eye shut on one face
to make up Shiva's three.

They took turns at that, it was a good game
'Shabash,' he clapped, his gaunt hand
with knuckles cramped
like wildfowl perched in the kitchen eaves,
crouched tight over beams, broken tiles
swept with sunlight scraped from gooseberries,
musky fruit fuzz, stiff caramel-colored stalks

that cannot yield to mouth or palm
stinting eternity

Stuck like a hearse glimpsed
in the far corners of a picture
someone else has made with white-robed men
dragging the cart from church
dirt blowing in swirls, a horizon
of bamboo flat and dry as glue.

VI.

Time was a drift of wing, claw, vine,
petal, stalk, skin of her tongue,
skin of a python struck with poles, eyes mashed
where the men made a ring and beat and beat
scales tough, corrosive, making iron glints

Making a sky, a theatre of words that rotate and pound
the horizon, a scene doubling itself
sheer as rice paper shielding sun and moon
heart's catastrophe in an unequal play
no hand could ever script.

She stops, she loosens all her clothes
she strips herself of silks, cottons,
bangles, necklaces, pins, slips off her rings.

She kneels to touch
the molten stuff from the python's head
then open eyed, she steps into the gutted skin
dances on a bloodied thing
mirroring paradise.*

---

* Note: You ask how "Skin Song" came to be written. In the last few years, after my
daughter's birth, I turned to work on a series of poems about childbirth and its
aftermath. "Passion" was the first. At the same time, I was working on the long
poem, "Night-Scene, the Garden." It was performed Off-Off-Broadway, a poem
spoken between mother and daughter. As for "Skin Song," it is related certainly to
these other poems. It has to do with terror—at the death of a much-loved
grandfather, and the way words break out of the female body. And when I say
'break out of' I think I mean that. Words that come from the female body are an
eruption. For there is no canonical sanction for female writing and speech. As such,
the word becomes grotesque, just as the body is, after childbirth. "Vak" is "Word"
in Sanskrit, though its meaning is different from "Logos" in the Christian sense. In
this poem, which deals with menstruation and childbirth, I see the word made
flesh. The dance at the end is the woman's life, the poem.

Whose House is This?

With thoughts of childhood, longings well up. Worlds not re-alized, glimpsed in waking dreams, in visions. Sometimes these dreams lead to questions borne in the mind, meanderings of thought. What would it be like to have a house of one's own? A house where no permissions were needed? Where even to speak of permission would be odd, for after all the bramble out-side the window ledge, the tree by the brick wall unfurls into sunshine the precise temperature of the skin. A belonging where one need not speak of such, where the hand can reach out and touch without withdrawing in shame or fear. Where matters of the heart may be spoken of proudly, where speech can be true. A woman's house, a house filled with women. Without madness, without deceit. A house for men. For children, too. A house filled with the hum of thousands of voices, small fires burning in the stoves where green mangoes and the bitter gourd are cooked. A house filled with the hum of syllables, long lines of silken sen-tences, snarls of commas, burrs of full stops. But how fragile such a house feels, held in the mind's space, tilting with the winds of desire.

Soon after I came to America, I wrote two poems about houses. When I look back in my journal, I find I have composed them side by side over a space of weeks, the two streams flowing on distinct sides of a page. Each house is a part of me. Or part of what I feel I must bear witness to.

"House of a Thousand Doors," the title poem of a book I published in 1988, is a dream poem. The house rises up in the pure space of the mind, as a dream might. Yet the elements that compose the house are drawn from the teakwood and brass of which my mother's ancestral house in Niranum is built. There are paddy fields around that ancient six-hundred-year-old house. The central structure, built around a courtyard filled with sand, is raised, higher than an infant can crawl, higher than a snake might be tempted to rise. The woman in my poem, a grandmother figure, is barred entry from the house. Why? Because she is female, because a married woman must leave her mother's house and go to her husband's home, where she can never be a daughter again. A species of exile is enjoined on her. But these explanations are not the poem, the poem is the music that rose in me, as I came here, a newly married woman to North America. Like "Hotel Alexandria," this, too, was a product of my living here.

"Hotel Alexandria" I think of as my first American poem. Not literally, but in spirit. I saw what transpires in the poem from a room I had rented on 103rd Street to have the quiet in which to write. I thought of the room as a place of privacy where I could sit and think or simply write for an hour or two, without interruption. One day, I bent over the windowsill and watched what was happening in the street beneath. What I saw turned into a prose poem. I was helped, too, by the music from a saxophone that wafted up to me. I called the piece "Hotel Alexandria" after the building that was being torn down from the inside and remodeled as a condominium. The poverty-striken families, the drunkards, the addicts who lived there were all being evicted. The pain of homelessness brought out in the rocking figure of the old bag lady was something I could not escape from. 'Read your Broadway poem,' people have said to me from time to time at readings. In its own way, the poem has found an audience. There is a way in which it contains 'news' of the world. Her flesh, her voice entered into me, a woman dispossessed in this crowded city, the great metropolis of North America. When I look back, I think of these two poems, "House of a Thousand Doors" and "Hotel Alexandria," as portals to my life, entry into a new world.

House of a
Thousand Doors

This house has a thousand doors
the sills are cut in bronze
three feet high
to keep out snakes
toads, water rats
that shimmer in the bald reeds
at twilight
as the sun burns down to the Kerala coast.

The roof is tiled in red
pitched with a silver lightning rod,
a prow, set out from land's end
bound nowhere.
In dreams
waves lilt, a silken fan
in grandmother's hands
shell colored, utterly bare as the light takes her.

She kneels at each
of the thousand doors in turn
paying her dues.
Her debt is endless.

I hear the flute played in darkness,
a bride's music.
A poor forked thing,
I watch her kneel in all my lifetime
imploring the household gods
who will not let her in.

Hotel Alexandria

Corner of Broadway and 103rd Street. I stand in the cold staring at Alexandria Hotel, a hospice the city kept its poor in. They're dismantling it now, tearing out pipes, bricks, even the tiles that lined the dingy basement. Two men carry out a sofa; it has black and blue stripes on the arms. Next, a mirror with the gilt impossibly intact; a pitcher with a broken lip no one will ever wash from. The sidewalk bristles with roaches.

There's barely room for the old woman who approaches, three plastic bags bound to her thighs, a man's jacket slung to her breasts, a woolen blanket someone threw out years ago covering her head so that only a tangle of hair shows. Hair acrid as salt. Newspapers are tucked in under her jacket. I see their rims, wasted with cold, fluttering.

She kneels on the icy ground, and rocks back and forth. A weird rocking creature. The blanket sags over the ground. Where did she come from? Grown jittery, the men yell at her, then turn back to their job. Back and forth, back and forth she rocks. The men return with a pile of pipes, bent, tips soiled with smoke. I see a skirt now, under the plastic bags, a cotton skirt printed with half-moons. At least her flesh is covered. The rusty pin on the jacket holds. The rocking creature has no gloves. She does not moan.

'Whose house is this?' I dare not cry, for a Chinese couple pass me by, their bedding rolled up in canvas. They have crossed the red lights with great care, looking right and left, left and right. They notice me, standing here, my soles leaking black water. I am two weeks old in this city. I have come here by subway. Memory drew me here, the danger of the unlit passage.

I knew that the white gulls that crowd the broken walls of the Alexandria Hotel would not cry to me, yet I had come as if drawn to the ground of my making, a house dismantled, the poor shed to the streets of Manhattan.

Alexandria, city of my childhood, where seagulls wheeled over the burning waters and I thought them angels. Where old couples, Muslim and Copt, carried out their bedding and laid it to sun. Where children cracked sesame seeds in their teeth and laughed at the gulls that hovered over Farouk's abandoned palace. Alexandria, where tongues of water rose and kissed my face: let me speak now, in this cold air, of the blisters of birth. My voice imprecise, my ignorance that of a perpetual immigrant, a woman with nowhere to lay her head.

Sidi Syed's Architecture

I sometimes wonder what he was like
Sidi Syed, a small man
come all the way from Abyssinia,
his skin the color of earth
before the waters broke loose
from the Sabermati river.
It was Ahmed's city then, in the year 1500.

Loitering by the river
he watched infants with blackened eyes
swinging in their cradles,
mothers with chapped hands laundering.
He saw skins of cattle and deer
laid out to dry
on the sharp rocks;
heard voices in them calling him,
crying out
as if home were nothing
but this terrible hunger
loosed between twin earths,
one underfoot by the river bed,
the other borne in the heart's hole.

Sometimes at night
did fear catch hold,
a shadow dragging its own robes;

water trapped in its own
unutterable weight?

Well before his death
a great man now
reimbursed for service of the Shah,
he picked the hands of a master cutter.
From crags of marble
he watched it grow
on driest land, no tract of water near,
the threshold lightly raised
to slipping lines
a corset to the hips of finest stone
arched to a tympanum so rare
it fled from nature.
Was it for him
this starry palm
with vine on vine still tumbling,
a tumult of delight
struck from a stonecutter's hands?
Fit elaboration of a man unhoused
yet architect of himself,
his genius still smouldering?
The mosque was hollow though
like a sungod's tomb;
it tracked his hunger
the madness of stretched skin
still so close
on those noisy river beds.

Tangled Roots

In my quest for an imaginative source sufficient to withstand the pressures of life in a new world, I made up a grandmother figure. I needed her ancestral power in a world where so much of what I knew myself to be was hidden, veiled, could not appear. Through such a figure I might be able to cut through to the soil of my life. In order to live in this new world I needed to cut through into the rich loam of my earliest sensations and practices. Language was part of the problem. If indeed English, 'the rough basement,' as William Blake calls it, had covered over the roots of my being, and in the depths of my soul I did not doubt this, then I needed what lay at hand—pickaxe or shovel or sharp stones— to cut through into the earth. In her novel, *Ceremony*, Leslie Marmon Silko writes of an older woman who struggles to reconcile her family with the larger community, but finds that the instinct of gathering together scattered emotions and needs into 'a single prayer bundle that would bring peace to them all' doesn't work anymore. Something else has gotten in the way. The older in-gathering of longing and desire, indeed of human practices, no longer functions. What has become of these deep matters of the heart? 'The feelings were twisted, tangled roots and all the names for the source of this growth were buried under English words, out of reach.' Though I had not read Silko's work at the time I wrote these poems, I think it was a similar instinct that gripped me. Perhaps, through the figure of an older woman, the rich vein of being could be tapped, the roots touched, healed.

I drew on what I knew, what I had in my thoughts and my memories. And I fused into her being the radically disparate facets of grandmothers known and unknown haunting me. At moments there was a savagery that, even as it opened up, flowed into words, threatened to annihilate my separate, distinct self.

Like everyone else I have two grandmothers. My mother's mother, who died before I was born, was Elizabeth Kuruvilla. She was born in 1884 and was active in the Nationalist movement, an ardent follower of Mohandas Gandhi, and the first woman member of the Legislative Assembly in Travancore. As a young woman she had studied in Madras, gained an M.A. in English Literature, and taught briefly at Presidency College. She traveled widely, all over India, to Europe, and to China. The portraits of her in my mother's house, the broad, high forehead and dark eyes, haunted me. I tried to imagine what it might have been like to be born into that era of upheaval, to find one's voice as a woman.

My father's mother, Mariamma, the grandmother I knew, lived in the old house in Kozencheri. A tall, strong woman, she spoke very little. But she ruled that household on the hill with an iron fist. In all the years that she was alive, she hardly left her husband's property. And how little she spoke, my grandmother, how words stuck in her throat. She was the daughter of a philosopher and scholar of Sanskrit in Kottayam, who for all his learning was not a great believer in the cause of women's education. My grandmother knew how to read and write, that was the extent of the book learning she was given. She was married off young.

How different they were, these two grandmothers. I struggled to figure out how each could be part of me, the woman in the public world, the other held within the traditional sphere of domesticity, barely stepping out of her house. Both were born into an era of great social change for women in India, yet how differently their lives had marked them.

A few years after I arrived in this country, I lived for six months in a Midwestern town. I was invited to visit the creative writing class at the university. The project was innocuous enough. The professor was discussing poems and coming upon some of mine in a journal decided to use them. The class had already read the poems, and I was invited to come and respond to questions. One of the poems they had picked was "Poem by the Wellside." There was an old, old woman in it. I was nervous, never having set foot in an American creative writing class, though as a student in Britain and a teacher in an Indian university I had heard rumors that such classes existed in North America. I tried to start off as best I could, in low-key fashion. Most questions I responded to with 'perhaps,' 'yes, if you think so,' 'you may well be right,' the sort of noncommittal responses I imagined would be innocuous. Certainly these seemed to work when I was asked about specific points of meaning in the poems, the cultural base of images and so forth. When pressed, I insisted that my readings of my own poems were no more privileged than anyone else's, something I actually believe.

In this way, I was able to preserve myself at what I thought was a cool, comfortable distance. The talk turned to "Poem by the Wellside." A middle-aged woman to my right—I had noticed her earlier; she had seemed tense, anxious to speak—suddenly broke out: 'She wants to kill you, don't you see?'

'Kill me? Who?'

I was aghast, hardly trusting myself to words.

'That old Indian woman in your poem, don't you see that?'

I sat in a stunned silence. All I remember is the class breaking up. I got up, smoothed my skirt, chitchatting as best as I could with the professor who had invited me.

For two whole nights I could not sleep.

Did the old woman want to kill me? Was it in the poem? I remembered having written in response to the old woman's cries the lines:

'I will not turn to her/ I will not perish.'

Why had I written the lines, what did they mean? And in any case, why think that killing entered into it? I was scared by the student's question and by her tone of utter certitude.

Why should the old woman glimpsed in water want to kill me? Was it the past rounding back? I did not ask myself those questions. The gash of dislocation was too fierce.

The composition of a poem is both evasion and discovery, and what one discovers while writing or in its aftermath cannot be carted about and displayed at will, as a precious ornament might. Its truth might be too unsettling by half.

In any case, the image of truth as retention doesn't work for me. I prefer the notion of loss, composition structured by loss. By stripping something, losing something, I touched her, that savage, fearful old mother. And perhaps by this point she was not my grandmother at all, not a real figure, portion of my ancestry. Rather a darkness in the soul, glimpsed through water.

In part of what was to become the long poem "Night-Scene, the Garden," I wrote of a boat trip the whole family took when I was a little girl. An eclipse of the sun was foretold. In great excitement, we set off in a little boat from Kochi harbor. In the poem I imagine the boat tipping over and the grandmother figure, all made up in my head, gripping me hard, as the water rose over us both. I then wrote the lines I needed to: 'When they pulled/us out/we would not/come unstuck.'

Why could we not come unstuck?

Because we are one flesh, she and I, a heartbeat skipped in time. Because I can hear her within me. Because of my mother tongue, which is pure speech, which I maintain in its uncluttered state in my head by virtue of living in North America hardly speaking it at all. Because grandmothers speak and die, and grandfathers believe in immortality. Because I write in the script of a colonial language, which I must melt down to my own purposes.

I was taught my mother tongue by highly literate people, but because I was schooled in the Sudan, I was able to avoid learning the script of Malayalam. And when, during my trips to Kerala, the tutor arrived, I would run away. Somehow Sanskirt did not bother me so much, so as a child I learnt a few lines, a few syllables. Malayalam seemed too close. Later, when I started writing poetry, the prospect of learning a script that might overwhelm the world of my earliest memories was fearful to me. My mother tongue remains in that sense at the level of speech and dream, yet people have told me that the rhythms of my poetry owe a great deal to Malayalam—the patterns of sound, alliteration, assonance—and this always pleases me.

The rightness of English sounds, however, was a different matter. Just as my mother was sent off to a boarding school in India run by Scottish Presbyterian ladies—she was just seven at the time—and her mother was too busy with political work to take care of a young girl—the place was Spartan: no mirrors, simple mats, a strict regimen of prayer—so I, a whole continent away, two and a half decades later, now under my mother's resolute domesticity, was committed to a tutor also Scottish, who was to teach me proper English.

This lady, upright no doubt, taught me a strict concern for the proprieties: how to speak, how to hold a knife and fork, how to curtsey. It was never known when a crowned head might visit the erstwhile colony. I was six. Her plump, well-meaning face dazed me slightly. I was hooked and snared. There was nowhere to run to. Facing her, I learnt for myself the slight, secret animosity toward the English language my own mother has. From her nationalist parents, my mother learnt both a fluency in English and a sense that its colonial trappings had to be subverted. My father had no such problems. A scientist who studied in English, he is comfortable in no language, and when necessary, Malayalam serves him best.

As for myself, I am aware that the language I use most fluently, that I can shape and work with best, is rarely a language I dream in. That is, when my dreams have words to them. The gap, the cleft between wordless intimacy and functioning script, is coequal in intensity with the fissures in my daily life, the estrangements, the castings adrift I need as I write. And there have been times when I have thought of my labor as rather like transporting or ferrying across wordless, tangled thoughts and sensations into language. And the linguistic activities I commit myself to are, on the one hand, related to the simplest transactions an Indian woman might make, living here, habit easing the discomforts of difference, and on the other, to the perplexed, hesitant nature of poetic speech.

Poem by the Wellside

Body, you're a stranger here
I dare not touch the scars
of stippled flesh
milk left when it fled,
a dry worn belly,
palms filled with dark water.

Herbs: camomile, the boxed and sheltered rue
wild heliotrope (did mother touch
it to her cheeks so the sun
would kiss and not burn?)
melting, all melting in water.

I was seven when I bent the bough
and saw my face in well water.

Nightly as the bark cracks
an old hag
with herbs in her teeth
yells 'Meena!
Meena, my daughter.'

I will not turn to her
I will not perish.
My poem made in a cold country
is not about death.

But the blue of heliotrope is bitter;
rue, its stalks
plucked from my dreams
make a necklace of grief.

Will I kneel in this patch of sunlight?
Will I pray?

Severed from my birthplace, I hear my name
(she cried out my name through her
black teeth)
shed syllables
in air so tender
the sounds melt, twisting
sunlight in threads.

I cannot stop my tongue.
'Old woman,
will water pour from the well?
Will a stream of water take root,
make a table, a pitcher, a bowl, bread?

'I am hungry, old woman,
I must live!'

At dawn her voice turns
in the coil of my ear,
an ancient anonymity
savage as sunlight.

'We are poor,'
she whispers,
'women from a poor country.

'By the wellside
our dreams
drop their clothes
and flee.

'You can ask for nothing.
As for your belly
let it burn
as wild grass is burnt
at nightfall, in your mother's country.'

Boating

One summer's day
we put out in a painted boat
the family entire,
a few friends included

The men in dhotis and
well-fitted shirts
a few with cigars spouting smoke

The women with their saris
edging right past
their eyes, drawn down

Against the sun
that eclipsed itself in fury
at the Kerala coast.

We rocked at a rope's end
in Cochin harbor
till my great uncle Alexander
cried out, dropping his pipe

And the men screwed
monocles just right
and the women crouching down
held bits of broken mirror
to their eyes

Or clear grey glass
my grandmother
for me, crying
child, child
so the sun might kiss
and not burn

Child, unripe child

Till the wooden hill
dashed suddenly
against the swollen pier
and shot us
into cold sea spray

The blackest depths
drawn up in pleated waves,
my smocking dress
puckered and ripped with salt

Child, O child
shut your eyes
so tight

Grandmother cried
clutching me
to her bony neck

Her silken cloak
with the golden pin
stuck fast
to my fist

When they pulled
us out
we would not
come unstuck.

Her Garden

The mountains crackle
they are full of flint
the cicada bristles
it does not sing
in grandmother's garden
as mulberry trees
gnarled like her hands
start their long slide
seawards.

I imagine her sitting
under the mulberry leaves
hot fruit splashed
to her eyes,
a blindness cleaned

in that solitary hour
when trees clamber
out of bark
and swim
to a rock that is black
and bare
and like nothing
else in this homeland.

I like to think
she died in the day
her face set heavenward

exacting little attention
from the sun:
once risen it sets
in finicky chaos
in a sky so flat and blue
that light mirrors itself
as if on water, soundlessly:
so losing body
she crept into her own soul
and she slept.

As young goats leap over cracks
in the garden wall,
as the cicada shunts sparks
from its wings,
I remember her.
She died so long
before my birth
that we are one, entirely
as a sky
disowned by sun and star:
a bleakness beneath my dreams
a rare fragrance
as of dry mulberry
pierced by this monsoon wind.

Erupting Words

Through speech, the entanglement of thoughts and feelings might be unwound, the truth permitted to shine, however fitfully. To reach the grandmother figure, I had to lose body, touch death. And in poems, such as "Her Garden," I have written of this. But what if, instead of touching a dissolution, words absorb the body's revolt? Might there be something barbarous in this return to the flesh, desire's contingency overwhelming space?

What if this return to the flesh should revel in its crudeness, a coughing, guttural eruption, a spewing forth of the juices?

Perhaps Antonin Artaud best understood the necessity of such eruption. In his metaphysic of the body *in extremis*, he realizes its coughs, grunts, gasps, wheezes, groans as crucial to the self; a self in which the mind lives in the flesh, 'quick as lightening.'

Performance had to strip apart the given language, in order to reach the truth. If there is cruelty here, it is a necessary cruelty. In the postcolonial epoch, we can draw on Artaud's experiments. The English we must work with has to be torn apart, stitched together, so that, lit by our anguish, our joys, we return to the body of our thought. Not a first thought, for the illusion of the ordinary must be left behind. Rather, a thought that reveals snarled, even delirious historical processes. And in saying this, I allude to the individual psyche too. After all, what am I but all those other selves that compose me? Yet the question of madness, the final boundary of bodily performance, may be forced on us.

'Shelter, unhousedness, the multiple speeches that surround us, broken walls, prison cells. The thoughts turn jagged in me. Everything is overcrowded. Everything is emptied out. I dream of barbed wire.'

It is a few years now since I wrote those lines. I was looking out at the sweet delicacy of falling snow in upstate New York, the ribbed trunks of apple trees in the distance, the red flash of a child's sweater. The child was running through the snow. Where her tracks were, I saw barbed wire. It rose ghostly, commanding space. The western light was pierced by barbed wire. I saw the outer edge of the compound in my grandfather's house in Tiruvella, wire bedded into earth, then strung in loops of metal onto granite posts. Right by the barbed wire, I saw a woman. How familiar her face seemed. The traditional white garments pinned her in place, but her hair burst out in a phosphorescence that forced my eyes shut.

That night she invaded my dreams. Each coil of her hair was a living snake. A fierce and desolate power filled her mouth. Her mouth with all the unsaid words inside, was burning up the snow. O palimpsest of memory, I wanted to cry: what are we?

I could not bear it any more and wrote to my friend Susie Tharu, who lives in Hyderabad. She shares a Kerala background with me and I have always felt she understands my compulsion to write. Here are a few lines from the letter:

'...I am congenitally incapable of setting down facts, though that might ease life somewhat, and I strive instead for the meaning that has been driven underground and for music to make that meaning come back, closer to us, to the conscious mind, without fear, with a surcharge of knowledge...I saw C., you may have seen her near our home in Kerala. I saw her hair matted, her house filled with mud. This is so fearful to me. At the same time, there is such power in her...Remember you once wanted me to keep a daybook, bits, scraps and all? One has to have that knowledge. My poem is a groping toward it, darkly.'

The poem I was working on then, "Night-Scene, the Garden," stops with the vision of segregation, men and women cut apart, the men with books and spears, the women with cooking pots, their mouths bubbling prayers. The poet's head smokes. Alphabets are ablaze. After this terror, the Coda to the poem is conceived of as a sideways thrust, an ellipsis, making music for the purposes of sense.

And the madness that I worked into the vision of my aunt Chinna, a fictitious figure, where does that come from? It is an eruption, a breaking loose, something barbarous. But I see it as stemming from a woman's need to reach out, understand the whole universe as if it were a fruit glowing. A fruit burning in the sky as Hunuman thought the sun. Leaping, a woman might fly right into its radiance, setting her hair aflame.

Through writing, what is figured as excess, what burns, can be made to mark the whiteness of the page. Once in India, I wrote a play which I called *Woman Building Wall*. I do not think it was a particularly good play. In fact, even as I wrote it, I was aware that in a piece that needed to work against language, use gestures, bodily motion, there were far too many words. In part, the play was about the terror of an enforced marriage. But all through the action a woman was working, building a wall. A group of friends who were interested in avant-garde performance rehearsed it for awhile. After the group fell apart, I tried to lose the play, scatter the pages here and there. It must have been a case of right hand striking against left, for I quite forgot that I posted the text to the journal *Enact* in Delhi, where, several months later, Rajinder Paul published it.

My only other experience with performance was "Night-Scene, the Garden." Though written as a poem, it was performed Off-Off-Broadway by the Medicine Show Theatre Ensemble as part of their Spring 1989 series. I was invited to a rehearsal. I took the subway and at West Broadway came upon the flat metal doors to the theater. I remember Barbara Vann, the artistic director, guiding me forwards in the half darkness. We had first met over a cup of coffee weeks earlier and I was struck by her understanding of the poem: 'It's about houses, about generations,' she had told me. Now she led me forwards, flashlight in hand, toward white painted steps and a sudden flood of light. The players were rehearsing in a large room lit by enormous windows, cracked glass held in place by strips of tape. I thought of the lines in my poem:

Will it be hot like this on the other side of paradise?
Will the birth lines hold fast?

I sat at the edge of a large, overstuffed sofa, looking out at the bare windows and the flat terrace beyond. The performers had just started when I got up, nervous beyond belief. 'How can you possibly understand this? I mean without having seen that house, that well.' I heard my words echoing, collapsing. Barbara tried to reassure me, but the sandy courtyard of Tiruvella, the language of home seemed so very far.

Minutes later, the players started singing the opening of the poem, about nightbirds, and my heart rose into my throat. It sounded in their mouths, the music I had heard and not heard. As if paradise were here already in bird song, in ululations come from human mouths. I could not believe my words had anything to do with the sounds that came from their mouths. It struck me that the loneliness I live with in my writing life was being touched and eased in a tenderness I could not have imagined. When it got to the part in the poem about the house being dese-crated, emptied out, I felt as if my own body were tied to an ox, tugged over rough soil, hands broken open, ploughing that soil. After the sung part there was a discussion about the coda, how it should be voiced. What were Krishna's colors, someone asked.

So I sat there with the light streaming in through the win-dows onto the bare floor where they worked, bodies and voices struggling for a concordance of tone, breaking it up, starting all over again.

I felt my soul flow into the transition they made as they sang in the voices of women, birds, spirits. Afterwards, as I walked on Franklin Street, I saw the houses of Manhattan, bronze-piped chimneys, green-tiled roofs pitched as if the im-maculate clouds above the subway stop made a theater for us, our yearnings loosed from their hinges and jambs, raised weight-less, like banners freed in the sunlit air.

Aunt Chinna

Do you recall
your old aunt Chinna
the night you turned seven?

Hair all cracked with mud
hot and dried
she fetched more from the cobra's hole
in a little silver spoon.

It was her mind, child
after her father died
what was left for her?

Heaps and piles of sewing
every tiny scrap
she saved until the end,
samplers with little mottos
Honor thy Mother and thy Father
Home is best
and other such sayings
the English woman taught her.

She could slip the needle through
and knot the cotton, so little showed.
Sometimes her silk had the sheen
of a hummingbird's wing
flashing under the bent vine.

. . . .

In your grandmother's house
birds sang all night
the sky was a canopy of light.

The full moon of her love
bathed Chinna.

Chinna laughed like a two year old
cut jokes with father
about the price of candlewax or tobacco.

She had no one to care for her
when father died.
I grew to hate her too.

She'd filch
rolls of brocade from our dead mother's saris
set them in the sun,
stare at the knobbles of gold,
lumps and jots of gleaming silver
pinned into wheels of amethyst, turquoise and ruby

Sit and stare for hours
at those bumpy lights
as if the universe
had formed inside her mind.

Then came the mud,
her nightly fascination with it.
She raced, clothes streaming
from her sides, mud in her hair
like a stuck boar
uprooted from its pit,
all in public down the village street.

Your uncle Paulos almost hung her in his rage.

Once he gave chase with five armed men
he almost had a private army then,
the mahout I think snared her with his thong
thick as a man's neck.

Poor Chinna,
snooked like a wild chicken.
I hate to think of what happened to her.

All her stitching stopped.

She crouched
by the mango tree in its crust of dirt
hiding the coiled menstrual cloths,
the heaps of paper
on which she wrote her name

Over and over in all the languages
she thought the earth contained.
Bits from Revelation her favorite book,
songs like little children sing
when fever drives them under the mother's wing.

. . . .

One night she came and said to me
There shall be no more sea
or The sea shall cease
or some such thing.

I thought it was that boating
trip we took just before the sun's eclipse.
You fell into the water with mother

we had to change your clothes,
those pretty pink shoes with the shine on them
we bought from Bengali market,
ruined quite.

Mother trembled so,
with rage I think not knowing why the sea
behaved like that, a sudden wave and poof
all gone into black saltwater.

Well Chinna was there with us
though who'd have known?

She wore a pale grey sari
we gave her for the feast day after Lent,
her chin tucked in like a pigeon brooding,
her whole face hidden in the spray.

. . . .

Death seizes you in the morning
she sang to me
my mad aunt Chinna

Kneel
kneel she sang to me,
clutch the polished doorknob
lick the doorstep clean

Kneel
kneel she sang to me,
before they bind
your mouth with cords.

She broke into her babble
chattering of a dog

whipped at the master's gate

A woman's hand
unnaturally pale
severed in a rice bowl.

Twisting her cloak
in both her hands
she rocked
beside the silken bed

'O Saramma
I would have this girl child
laid naked
on rosewood.

'Touch her tongue
no, not with gold
as is our practice

'Take earth, dark mud
in both your palms
annoit her tongue
her tiny limbs.'

Tighter and tighter
she bound her clothes
about her, my mad aunt Chinna
rocking and rocking
by the rosewood bed

The fern leaves
mother set in a porcelain bowl
by the window ledge
to see if their spores
would hatch, fell to the floor

They clacked their tongues
about aunt Chinna's thighs
and would not stop.

Next morning
when the elders
took themselves to church
the ripe red berries
in the silver dish
took up the chorus

And their fruity gossip
lit up all the parlor.

Coda from Night-Scene

Threshold Song

In darkness, at the threshold
of a house laid waste
I stand, refurbishing a thought grown still

Wild bees have entered the rice cellar
a humming bird flits by the broken sill

Mortal acts cling closer now
all substance sucked out
spat as if by a hot wind
to the oddest rim of the physical

And the mind moves apart
washing its hands of everything
thinking it has all happened, all already.

Once the doorways were new
filled with incense smoke
the tang of crushed nettles

And the infant thrust past
her mother's bone
and the vagina unhooked its tongue
moaning in inhuman tone.

Now to understand the scuffed leaves
beside the steps,
curtains torn down
where they led the goats in
excrement piled high
in buckets in the kitchen

And by the ancient well
gravel, torn rocks
the reddening soil where voices have cried
in warrior tongues

Of axe and sword and nageswaram
and the high longing of men on elephant back.

. . . .

Glimpsed in Indigo

In midwinter
the grass is dry
round about my mother's house
and tiny seeds run riot.

Through a barred window
I watch the crow-pheasant edge close,
right claw hauled upwards
a fraction of an inch

Disturbing the tight span
of wing whose fierce blue
glimpsed from a half-light
melts into indigo
a kingfisher might covet

Lord Krishna's color

But the stickiness of seed
burst from old stalk
and borne on the wing
makes it a warm thing

Part of earth's treasure
soft and sore
clung to this garden wreath
this net of bone.

The bird touches its claw
to the rim of cloth
laid out to dry

Two saris
stitched with mild blue flowers,
hems starred with starch

A white lucidity
crusting in patches
as milk might
on the heavier globes of flesh.

Omana had beaten them on rock
dipped them in starch
from the blackened cooking pot

Wrung them out
and stretched them taut
against the crumbling wellside.

When the hot wind came
they rose in patches
like small sails lit

in unsubdued elation,
turning feverish as her strong hands
caught and clasped the shimmering stuff

Minutes later
she stretched them out,
flat beside the mango trees

No wrinkles visible
just the taut white stalks
that bore them up
a good half inch above the earth

And in the empty hold of air
whispers of children born into this garden.

Bordering Ourselves

'She says to herself if she were able to write she could continue to live.'

—Theresa Hak Kyung Cha, *Dictée*

A few years ago I wrote a book that I called *Fault Lines* and in it I kept puzzling over the borders shifting inside me—languages, gestures, memories of places. When people ask me, as they sometimes do, why I wrote that book, I have a hard time replying. Perhaps a book is like karma, the long line of fate to which one is attached, the scents of past lives flowing off the pages. I had a hard time with *Fault Lines*. Nightmares were part of my life as I composed it. I sensed very clearly that when I finished it, I too would be done for. Be run over by a car on Broadway, fall off the edge of the subway platform, that sort of thing. Something grand and final. Somehow, I seem to have survived.

Still, my existence was so marginal in the new world in which I found myself that I felt that having this book out in the world might give me the right to be in America. What an odd thing to think about a book or one's life for that matter. And what might it mean to have a right to live somewhere, anywhere? I started to muse on what we call "history." Did it mean a space memories can flow into, a depth of shared sense, of matters invisible that pierce our ordinary lives?

Having entered this world as an immigrant I felt I was living in a place where I had no history. Who was I? Where was I? When was I? Those questions, drawn from Samuel Beckett's *Unnamable* had an odd echo for me.

In my early days in Manhattan when my son was very little, I would take him in a stroller down the subway. It was hard maneuvering down the steps. Kindly folks would help now and then by carrying one end of the stroller. Once it was a Latino man. He smiled at me, spoke to the baby in a warm gush. I thanked him as he turned to me, right by the token booth. I heard the melodious flow of words, but did not understand the question. I shook my head. I could tell he was offended. Why wasn't I replying?

Finally, in desperation, I said, 'Indian, Indian!' and he nodded. At my ignorance. He had taken me for a woman who could speak Spanish, a Latina. Other times I have gone down the streets, unaccompanied, and been asked, often by people I took to be from the South Asian diaspora: 'Where are you from? Guyana? Trinidad? Fiji?' The jeans, the short hair all meant I might well be from elsewhere—that shifting, diffuse diaspora. Of course, when I wear a sari no one asks such questions. Those who might be concerned see it as a flag for 'Indianness...' India, that strange land, far away. Land of maharajahs and snake charmers and poverty so desperate it ends in the plague.

'Hindu, they called me Hindu, then threw eggs at me. A group of skinheads in a car. I ran all the way home,' one of my students told me. She was from a proud Muslim family, living at the edge of Queens. She was walking home late one night from a movie, this young woman who I shall call Rumana, though that's not her name. Her name does not matter, but she might be you or I. What she went through matters terribly. Rumana had to figure out how to live her life after that episode. How to walk the streets, how to enter public space.

One is marked by one's body, but how is one marked?

'What wonderful English you speak,' a young woman of South Asian origin is told, a woman in her twenties, utterly American I would have thought. 'Where are you from?' they ask her next. She wonders how she can speak of that small town outside Detroit she calls home. It is very common for young Asian Americans to be asked for their land of origin whereas a young man or woman of European origin would never be asked the question in quite that fashion. He or she would pass, unerringly. Though what such a person from Latvia or Ireland feels deep down inside is another matter. After all, whatever the color of one's skin, memories of dislocation can be deeply 'othering.'

So what might it mean to pass in America? For an Asian American to pass? For some of us, it means making it in economic terms, assimilation translated into doing well, very well, not just making do. But the streets lined with gold are hard to walk and what happens with the heart can give one pause.

Once, in a small writing workshop for students at a prestigious eastern university, there were twelve of us in a high room. I listened carefully as a young Korean-American student told me of the club his wealthy father took him to, how his father told him to behave impeccably, lifting up knife and fork just so, how coming home the father burst into rage at what he saw as the son's lack of culture.

'And all the while,' the student told me, his eyes red with the strain of remembering, 'I could see how he was so mad at being in the place he was. But what could I do?'

Does passing mean being granted free passage? After fifteen years in this country I now have an American passport. It has a color photo of me, clearly different from the black and white I had in my Indian passport, and the background to the image is a honeycomb pattern in sugary pink, blue, and navy, quite a surprise. With this passport I can travel across borders, enter this country without visa or green card. But what if I don't have the passport on me? And what difference will the passport make to my concern about walking on country roads where no other people of color are to be seen? My fear of coming across men in army camouflage, toting rifles to kill deer, all the xenophobia of America sitting squarely on them, or bikers on Route 23 with big signs pasted to their machines: '500 Years after Columbus, Keep out Foreign Scum!'

In the city, I live close to Harlem. Sometimes when I walk up 125th Street I feel I am in another country, the shouts and cries, the passing figures, the small shop fronts in the old black neighborhood. I feel quite safe picking out a cap or a pair of overalls. There is no harm here in not being white. But I am not Black either. 'Indian?' a man in a khaki vest asks me. I nod. He passes me the clump of green plantains I have paid for. He smiles at me. I can pass here. But what does passing mean? For Asian Americans, multiple ethnic borders are part of the shifting reality we inhabit.

The racial lines of black and white have been complicated by the layers of immigrants who have entered and are remaking this country. And we are part and parcel of a world of complex, often fluid allegiances. Ethnicity in such a world needs to be recast so that our moving selves can be acknowledged. Strolling through the streets of Jackson Heights, the El just behind me, blocking out part of the sky, I may feel quite at home, all the smells and sights of India, versioned, in fresh combinations, but I cannot live there either. The enticement of America is quite precisely in its dazzling multiplicity.

But such shifting borders, particularly when racialized, can be tormenting. Who am I? When am I? The questions that are asked in the street, of my identity, mold me. Appearing in the flesh, I am cast afresh, a female of color—skin color, hair texture, clothing, speech, all marking me in ways that I could scarcely have conceived of. And there is a febrile edge to this knowledge, something that has always been with me, even in India, the country I 'come from,' a country where the issue of race never touched me. Yet years ago, living in Hyderabad, in my very early twenties I wrote a poem. Somehow the thoughts and feelings return to me: the danger of being seen in the street, the danger of being a writing woman.

Her Mother's Words

If you sit in a dark room
no light behind you
no one passing in the street can see
my mother said to me.

I sit in a dark room
a small lamp beside me
how should I write these lines
without a light, how should I see?

I asked myself
not knowing that the street
had such a vision of my woman's soul
as I should scarcely understand.

Now I know
my hands grow cold and
sight spills out of me.

Perhaps I should have said 'body' instead of 'soul' I now think, but then I correct myself. It is woman as prisoner of her sex that touched me, a difficult awareness that once led me to a study of Mary Wollstonecraft, writer, revolutionary, radical feminist.

But the borders here are different, the edges blurring. I am Indian here, in a way I never was in the subcontinent, in a way I never needed to be. And my femaleness is complicit with a racialized awareness. There is also the possibility of 'passing'—of entering, if only fitfully, into multiple worlds.

But the mind slips to the darkness on which such a possibility is built: Nella Larsen's world, female selves unraveling in the haste to 'pass.' Her agile, anguished heroines come to mind: Helga Crane in *Quicksand*, Clare Kendry in *Passing*. Invented almost seventy years ago, these fictional women are torn apart by being African American in a racist world. Larsen's vision is tragically divided: on the one hand is the crowd, the dark thronging masses, the 'hordes,' one's own people rendered alien, a source of pollution. On the other hand is a white world, which might grant one exotic status. In Denmark, one might be a bird of rare plumage; in America, a gypsy or an Italian. Multiple imagined ethnicities draw these women forward, but blackness, borne deep inside, a fiery implosive, forces them to their tragic fates. Passing in a racialized world offers no harbor and the self, site of so many invented identities, must perish. Though anonymity, the tearing apart of the bonds of the past and family, might seem to allow for radical self-invention, Larsen was acutely aware of the quicksand of such an existence.

I grew up in what might loosely be called the postcolonial Third World. I grew up in two different countries, India and the Sudan. Multiple borders were part of my ordinary reality. In Khartoum as a young girl, I could sometimes pass for Sudanese and this was always a comfort to me. Though deep down inside, borne within me like contraband, was the knowledge I was Indian. That my grandparents lived in Kerala, where both my parents were born and brought up, a land of temples, churches, and paddy fields, quite unlike the stark desert and sandstone that one found in Khartoum. In those heady years of Sudanese democracy, my friends were experimenting with the tob. Some decided to wear the traditional covering, others found freedom outside it. Femaleness, then, at least in its external markers, could be negotiated. I understood, too, that what a woman chose to wear could be quite deceptive. Assia Djebar writes of how the veil can allow women a subversive entry into public space. While Djebar's Algeria is far from this country, one can learn from her analysis of the danger of the moving body. Her vision, forged at the time of the anti-colonial struggles in Algeria, sharpened her sense of the multifarious, covert shapes a female body could take, and what contraband, literally explosive, could be hidden under female coverings. Drawing on her knowledge, one can reflect on a female body crossing the domestic border, entering public space. And indeed such crossings can have a truly communal valency. Here, now, in America, we can reflect on such complexities, understanding that even as time and localities shift, there is very little we can take for granted as we etch ourselves in complex palimpsests of knowledge and desire. Identity politics, in other words, or what commonly passes under that appellation, gains in power to the extent that it is anchored with multiple lines to a common, if shifting, social reality.

Several years ago, I gave a poetry reading at Tufts University with Marilyn Chin. I remember Marilyn reading her poem, "The Barbarians are Coming":

'If you call me a horse, I must be a horse.
If you call me a bison, I am equally guilty.'

I felt myself grow quiet as she read those lines. Then I read my poem, "Ashtamudi Lake":

'Arawac or Indian
the names confine
there is nothing for us
in the white man's burden...'

In our different ways, both Marilyn and I were talking about living in America.

Talking? Is that a good word to use for a poet's speech—that heightened, intimate vocalization; why not? Surely poetry is as much speech as any other form of address. Both poems draw the hard power of naming, and of being named as Other, into the seams of the present.

After the reading, as people milled about, taking tea, helping themselves to sandwiches, a young woman came up to me. She beckoned, drawing me toward the window. When we were safely out of earshot of the others, she pointed at my sari:

'Can you really wear that here?'

'Why not?' Out of the corner of my eye, I saw the windowpane. Sunlight gleaming on the polished wood, but outside, in glittering heaps, soft as sugar, the snow.

'Not because of the cold, you mean?'

She shook her head. I can see her still, that young woman with her hair cut straight across her face in bangs, her worried eyes. 'They told my mother she couldn't.'

'Your mother?'

She nodded. In the background a tea cup fell to the ground. There were students milling about, sandwiches in hand.

'What does your mother do?'

'She's a doctor on Staten Island; she was told she'd have to wear a dress in the hospital. Can you wear that all the time?' She asked, touching the pallu of my sari.

'All the time I want. I guess I'm lucky where I work.'

'The ethnic thing is not a fault?' I felt the sense of shame in her.

'No, no,' I murmured, reduced almost to tears. And I put out my hand and touched her wrist.

I wanted to draw off the six yards of silk I had draped over my body, wheaten-colored silk, a gift from my mother in India. I wanted to show the young woman the gleaming length of the sari, then let the fabric flutter out of the window, as a banner might, signifying some hidden, transient joy passersby could only guess at. Suddenly the snow seemed ever so close, beautiful, blinding. And I wondered what it would be like to walk through the snow, all borders erased, skin tingling, eyes filled with blue skies of Somerville.

Ashtamudi Lake

I.

Approaching you
I skirmish with disaster

Bridges flee from me:
the spun steel of Brooklyn
Manhattan's avenues of metal

I am speeding over
Ashtamudi Lake

Where the train toppled in
where girls in white
a whole year later
tossed flowers

In a death ceremony
for corpses unshriven
swarming in water

If someone sings
an elegy
I do not hear it.

II.

In the carriage
I read a sign in Hindi first
Aag then in English
Prevent Fire

At Kayankulam the fish plates
lie in a stack
worn doors ripped
massed in a shining heap

Dragged from underwater
carriages rust
on their sides
immense as poorhouses

Innards beaten out
with chisel and hammer.

III.

Twelve years ago
I fled a mirrored room

Money plants on the sill
an Englishman's love seat
and four-poster complete
with striped furbelows—
Percy's Hotel, Secunderabad.

Earlier that day
across a table crushed
with friends I glimpsed you
for the first time

I set my hand in yours
I followed you
into your room

But as you stood
against the bed
I fled, confused, stricken

I could not trust
a thing so molten.

IV.

Now a hot rain falls:
our histories are hinged
a wooden post, a door
into a rambling house,
cracked unfinished architecture

A nation feting itself
on a forty-second anniversary
with gunfire on whitewashed colonnades
drumbeats in shore temples
forced marches past prison and penitentiary

Anthems on quarried slopes
where children crouch, picking
stones from rice
under guava trees stooped
with sunlight.

V.

At Kayankulam
in wayside stations,

bus halts where hot tea is sipped
from thick ceramic cups

Quick figures of our past subside:
a portico collapsed
built with cheap concrete—
two children on their way
to school barely escaped

Dust settles on the shrines
for sacred ones
St. George with spear and dragon

A goddess with four arms
hands lavish with paint
gripping rubies, lotus, lute
a stack of rupee bills

Billboards for ceramic
toilet bowls lilac and pink
posters for the latest
True Life Movie—a girl

Paper thin, leapt into water
as backdrop to her tiny hands
and face, two men, father and lover
mustachioed, muscular
erect in white dhotis.

Blunted by the processionals
of sight and sound
taxis with loudspeakers advertising
Coconut Oil Shampoo, Tutorial Colleges
that prepare you for Dubai

We forget the hands
of men and women raising
corpses from lakes, stones
for a new highway over
the flooded paddy field

Hands that scoop
ash from cooking fires
lit by the rim of Ashtamudi Lake
with stubble, dried sticks
bloodied gauze thrown out
from the local hospital.

VI.

Nothing stands still:
through the clatter of iron
wheels, wooden shacks, corrugated roofs
whirling by, I cry

What Vasco da Gama saw
in 1498 is fit to burn

Seeking spices and Christians
he came upon this coast
his blunt eyes glimpsed
territories edged with swords
the outposts of conquest.

Out of Europe's pitch heart
her Papal Bulls
the surreal sense of Empire
Henry the Navigator scrawling
on parchment, his compass
packed with steel
came the ships, the menace.

Columbus heading west
dreamt of the Indies
the gentleness of the natives
when he struck earth
appalled him: they greet us with
affection, he wrote, they would
make good slaves; in their ignorance
they pick up swords by the blade
their hands trickle blood.

Arawac or Indian
the names confine
there is nothing for us
in the white man's burden

With shards of sense
fissured, twice-born verbs
our history knits itself.

VII.

But who can bear the truth
of her life or his?

Pressed to the barred window
as the train rocks over steel

I think: the cold of Brooklyn
is inconceivable here
yet here too the body's heat
is stored in small things

Jade against the throat
a honey colored freckled fruit
set to the lips, a mark

your ring left on my palm
twelve years ago.

In a glass
in a speeding train
I see your face again
mirrored in mine

Outside is Ashtamudi Lake
on its surface
little is visible:

Fractures of light
a few reeds, floating stubble

The magnets death makes of us all
(the bonus of truth, call it that
if you will), a conquest

Rubbing raw the nervous
interstices of sense

Desire's nuptials lit in us
no elsewhere here
Only a house
held by its own weight
in the mind's space

Its elegant portico
of polished teak
tilting in heat

As we seize a door
with an ivory knob
and come upon flames.

I look back at "Ashtamudi Lake" and think: what would it be like to live in a house filled with flames? It is a question linked to another: what would it be like to walk naked, through the snow, into the shining air?

The shining blue that exists in the imagination, a sheer and brilliant nothingness, forces us back onto the fraught compact between body and language.

And sometimes it seems to me that it is only in the teeth of violence that we can speak the unstable truths of our bodies.

I think of Bensonhurst in Brooklyn, of Jersey City and the racist murders there. In Jersey City an Indian man was beaten to death, Indian women who wore saris or buttus were stoned by skinheads. I think of Hyderabad, Meerut, Delhi, Bhagalpur, and the communal riots and murders in those cities, as well as in the countryside of India. I think of the destruction of the Babri Masjid in Ayodhya. I think of the terrible bombardment of Iraq during the Gulf War, the countless quick and slow deaths, the massacres of children from on high under the gleaming aegis of the latest fighter-bombers.

What becomes of memory? What is obliterated? What is cast out? For this was also an Asian war and there were thousands of men, women, and children in the refugee camps set up in the Jordanian desert. I heard of a woman from Kozencheri who gave birth in the sand, then was airlifted, with others from neighboring villages, back to Kerala, in a wide-bodied plane, hundreds cramped together, cast out of Kuwait and Iraq, thrust back into India, into overcrowded houses, into temporary shelters.

Translating Violence

How do multiple anchorages work in the light of ethnic extremism? I am thinking of the destruction of the Babri Masjid in India on December 6, 1992 and the way in which Hindu extremism has coarsened the very fabric of the nation, the ways in which tiny ripples from that violent eruption worked into the diasporic community here.

On a cold, damp day, I rode out with a group of other Indians to a small town across the Hudson River. After the choke hold of traffic in downtown Manhattan and the dim half-light of the Holland Tunnel, came the New Jersey Turnpike and acres of industrial marshland, smokestacks and bits of old machinery, the greyness of earth and sky, till suddenly we turned and stopped in front of a small, low-lying motel that housed the Akbar Restaurant. The irony of the Bharatiya Janata Party (BJP) meeting in a restaurant named after the great emperor Akbar, who espoused the ideal of religious tolerance, was not lost on us. Inside the restaurant, the BJP was hosting a Friends of India fund-raiser. In the biting cold outside, protesters lined the muddy bank between road and parking lot, with raised placards reading 'Hindu-Muslim Bhai-Bhai,' 'Rebuild Babri Masjid,' and 'Stop Funding Massacres in India.'

In the closed conference room of the restaurant, Sikander Bakht, the BJP speaker who had come all the way from India especially for the occasion, spoke warmly of the virtues of Hindutva, the cultural priority of Hindus, the indissoluble bond between Hindu identity and Indian nationalism. Cries of 'Ram Rajya' raised by men, some of whom wore the red armbands of the Rashtriya Swayamsevak Sangh (RSS), echoed in the closed room. The speaker's plea to the listeners, not to forget their Indian identity, had not gone unheeded. Now an Indian identity seemed, in that hot, closed room, to rest on the destruction of difference, on the excision of all others who were not Hindu. If they had their way, the secular tradition, the rich, multiethnic character of India would be expunged forever.

One of the members of the Mosque Committee told me he was thrown out of the lobby outside the meeting room and threatened by the local police with handcuffs and the lockup if he resisted. While two carloads of police watched warily, some of the BJP group came out of the motel and two sets of Indians confronted each other on American soil. The riots in Bombay and in Surat were fresh in our minds. The bloodletting of Partition was just behind us. Was India to revert to that again? Would mosques, temples, churches, houses, schools have to be destroyed at whim, just because there was a prior claim on the soil? The irony of the BJP speaker, inside the Akbar restaurant, invoking Mahatma Gandhi's name was not lost on us. How long did one have to live somewhere to make it one's home anyway? Was there no protection for minorities anywhere?

It seemed quite appropriate to protest, to carry on this line of questioning on the democratic soil of New Jersey. The claims to identity that were made within the closed room of the Akbar Restaurant were heard by men and women who in their daily lives were hardly members of a Hindu majority, but were living as Asian immigrants, a not too visible minority in America. Why could they not feel the predicament of minorities in their own homeland? Why this terrible need to claim one cultural identity, singular and immovable, for India?

One of the members of the protest group, shivering in the sudden wind, spoke of the 451 Palestinians expelled by Israel, living in makeshift tents in southern Lebanon. 'It's cold there, too,' she said, smiling bitterly as the cries of 'Down, down, BJP' grew louder and the cars, filled with party supporters, eased out of the parking lot.

'What rights do we have anywhere?' she asked me. 'How will you write this?'

I smiled back at her wryly and stamped my feet, trying as best I could to free myself of the dampness. My toes were frozen and thoughts of writing were far from me.

Like many others, I had grown up at the borders of violent conflict. My mother's parents were Gandhians, believers in satyagraha, the way of nonviolent resistance. But even as stories of peaceful resistance in the face of lathi charges and mass arrests filled my ears as a child, there were also mutterings about the Indian National Army, of women who armed themselves, of others too, like Preetilata Wadekar, who threw bombs at the British.

The struggle to decolonize took on a different hue in my years of growing up in Khartoum. There was a civil war raging in the south of the Sudan, and students at the university who came from there would tell tales of torture and mutilation. As I left the Sudan to go to study in Britain I was well aware of the struggles for justice that raged on. In India at the time, there were students my age who joined the Naxalite movement; many others were sympathizers in the cause of armed struggle for justice. National independence was clearly only a very small first step and violence, in its multiple forms, would have to be confronted.

The struggle for women's rights flowed side by side with the postcolonial struggles for freedom. Even as the girlfriends I grew up with in Khartoum marched with men in the streets, demanding a solution to the 'Southern Question,' so those voices strengthened were raised against the horrors of clitoridectomy and varying personal decisions were taken on the tob, whether to cover oneself in it or not. In India, where I returned in the early '70s, a powerful feminism that sought to rewrite the nation in terms of a viable existence for women was taking shape. Friends in Delhi organized against bride burning; friends in Hyderabad collected the stories of women who were active in the armed uprising of the Telengana movement. Within me, too, was the awareness that Mohandas Gandhi, the apostle of nonviolence, in the course of his experiments in community living, both on Tolstoy Farm in South Africa and in Sabermati Ashram in Ahmedabad, had cut off the hair of young women he suspected of sexual misconduct. What place did women have, I wondered, in the new world?

The complexities that underlie female existence need to be set in relation to the constraints of power, both patriarchal and colonial. It is through such constraints that the woman's voice pits itself, translating violence. In his essay, "Representative Government" (1861), John Stuart Mill made the case for despotism. The natives of India were on his mind: 'a vigorous despotism is in itself the best mode of government...to render them capable of a higher civilization.' The strictures of colonialism and patriarchy fuse in this belief in the necessary exercise of despotic power, an argument that I sometimes heard voiced in the postcolonial world I grew up in, fused though with a sense of the need to keep women in their place, teach them what to do. Though the details of the patriarchal argument were not voiced in the precise modalities of Victorian rationality—after all, in India the elaboration of female sexuality is complex, woven into the fabric of a hierarchical society—a colonial sense of maintaining power, of keeping order was critically present. And somewhere in there, too, as a undertone, was the grim feel of progress, a forward march into the new world. The regurgitation of Victorian rationality sat ill at ease, though, in a world where the bounding lines of behavior, both for men and for women, were rapidly blurring. And there was a curious lack of fit between the corset-like constraints of dead British rule (one thinks of a garment shredded, shrunk, stays torn and visible, but still held up to the living, growing body) and the nationalism that paradoxically permitted it to be voiced. Perhaps it is no accident that the version of Indian history British colonialism established, indeed required, for its legitimation is one that the Hindutva forces have used, in part, to build on: Golden Age of Hindu Rule—Barbaric Muslim Rule—Progressive British Rule. In each case, the 'Woman Question' had to be marshaled into line.

After the destruction of Babri Masjid and the riots that followed, one thinks: what the more extreme factions want is nothing less than restoration of a mythic Golden Age, whatever the bloodshed involved, with women standing in as the mothers of the nation-state, or like the fierce female orators Sadhvis Uma Bharati and Ritambara Devi, whose voices have been copied out onto countless tapes and distributed in households in India, crying out to raise the saffron flag on the Red Fort in Delhi, wipe clean the slate of history, a cry for a cleansing so pure that all the complexities of a multitudinous, multireligious past are wiped out and history remade in the apocalypse of the mind.

What sense can the fraught reflections of a multicultural feminism offer us? If to be female is already to be Other to the dominant languages of the world, to the canonical rigors of the great classical literatures of Arabic or Sanskrit or Tamil, to be female and face conditions of violent upheaval—whether in an actual war zone or in communal riots—is to force the fragmentation both of the dominant, patriarchal mold and of the marginality of female existence.

Indeed, such fragmentation can work powerfully into the knowledge necessary for a diasporic life, for the struggle for a multicultural existence in North America. Indian women's advocacy groups, such as Sakhi in New York and Manavi in New Jersey, are working quite precisely against both the inherited patriarchal mold and the pressures of racism in the new world. And for feminism it is crucial to embrace the secular multiculturalism that is threatened by political extremism. Can the democratic struggles in India work into an understanding of multiculturalism in the United States? There is no simple answer, but such an understanding is part of the challenge of a new praxis, part of the exhilaration of the future.

And the possibilities for female expressivity become multifarious, even verging on explosive. My mind moves back to the tattered corset of Victorian rationality evoked earlier. It is as if one picked it up and tried to fit it over a female body, vital, magnificent, with as many arms as the goddess Saraswati, and one of the arms, maimed from passage, still bleeding.

And how will our goddess speak? In many tongues, in babble, too, I think, mimicking the broken words that surround her, here, now, in America.

. . . .

The bitter translation of self required by violent conflict is clear in these writings by women from South and West Asia that I have been reading in the collection *Blood into Ink*. It is as if the continuous pressure of violence, always already localized, had forged itself into a second language—an Otherness more radical than any the woman writer had been forced previously to feel— and through this anguishing, potentially fatal medium, she must voice her passions, reconfigure her world.

Such expressive acts require fierce labor of the feminine imagination: the walls of domesticity broken down, the retaining walls of desire breached. In Mirdula Garg's powerful short story, "The Morning After," a middle-aged mother of two sons faces a mob in Delhi. The narrative is set during the 1984 riots after Indira Gandhi's assassination, when thousands of innocent Sikhs' were attacked and killed. Satto Auntie has hidden a young Sikh lad in her cupboard; helping him escape, she pays with her own life. In Ghada al-Samman's "Beirut Nightmares," realism is exchanged for surreal séances of a world in convulsion. As a 'Palestinian saboteur' is crucified outside, none of those who drink and dance inside the luxury hotel realize that the man being crucified is really the Messiah whose birth they think they're celebrating. Given the strenuous nature of such an aesthetic, it is hardly surprising that, at times, the rituals of terror overcome the everyday world and the otherness of violence seems to fill the substance of speech.

The very marginality of the female condition becomes highly charged in a world filled with conflict. Women can maneuver differently than men, and even fiercely partisan women can use their mnemonic powers, not to paint a nostalgic foyer from which the female self has been brutally evicted, but rather to fuse together fragments of a difficult world. Ancestral memory must be recast so that innocence, however frail, might survive. In Samira Azzam's story, "On the Road to Birak Sulaiman," the deep sense of belonging that the Arab family feels even as it is forced to flee ancestral lands is exploded by Israeli gunfire; and while the death of the young child has no possible consolation, nationalism, the naming of this land as ours, provides the narrator with a momentary hope: 'Look, this is a mountain. The day will come when we turn it into an Arab mountain.' The issues of territory and selfhood become intertwined.

Territoriality, then, in these postcolonial writings by women, becomes not just an issue of what Benedict Anderson has called the 'ghostly imaginings' of nationalism. It becomes a flesh and blood issue, literally flesh and blood. For it is through the border crossings undertaken by the female body, the living 'I,' that the creative potentiality of the world is inscribed afresh. In "Parbati" by Farkhanda Lodhi, the metamorphic nature of the female self is made visible. Crawling through the barbed wire into no man's land, Parbati changes her name, her whole identity refashioned under the heat of passion.

Her border crossing and return precipitate a questioning of woman's place in the already constructed world. Indeed, here, as in several of the other works, the radical disruption of life in the war zone permits an escape from the strict feminine mold of ordinary life, opens up explosive possibilities of freedom.

In Nuha Samara's "Two Faces, One Woman," the protagonist, left alone by her husband in war-torn Beirut, sits in front of a mirror and cuts off her long hair. As she bleaches it, she feels her face harden, feels she is beginning to look like a Nazi officer. She takes her old father to a hospital, she learns how to shoot, she takes a lover. The release of sexuality that both Lodhi's and Samara's protagonists feel signals a dissolution of the old patriarchal bondage, the radical possibility of female independence in a splintering world.

But what becomes of so-called 'normalcy'? How shall we continue to cross the street, wash vegetables, bring our children home from school, approach our lovers, bury our dead? Life needs to go on, particularly the kinds of ordinary care that stitches the world together. The contortions of the everyday caused by multiple forms of violence—bombardment, mass shootings, curfews, riots, rapes, the forced exodus of civilians—when crystallized into art, reveal not merely the extreme, enforced condition, but also the hidden structures of a world previously taken for granted, a world in which women have not often been at ease.

What does it mean to speak out in a time of violence? What becomes of the lyric voice fronting war? These are not questions to which quick answers can be found. But they are questions we are forced to ask ourselves at the tail end of the century, our earth torn up by multiple battles. Sometimes women's writing works through radical negativity and we are forced to witness the nightmarish logic of war, a surreal theater of cruelty that fractures identities, leads to the sudden irruption of sexual desire, small explosions of pleasure, or then again the body turned to a brutal instrument. At other times, the fragility of helpless children, the instinct for natural beauty, the tenderness toward all of existence that makes us truly human is illumined. At such times, the second language of violence only serves to force into visibility the longing for love.

In her poem from Beirut, Huda Naamani evokes the excess of cold: 'We will write our bodies with snow, the soul/remains a horizon.' But the voice continues in the longing for peace, for perfection: 'each stone we will heal/its wound, each grapevine we will prune/with our lashes... 'Amrita Pritam, a generation earlier in Punjab during Partition, noted peepul trees smashed, swings broken, the Chenab flooded with blood and cried out to her dead predecessor in the terrible hope that time might be remade:

'I ask Waris Shah today/To speak from the grave/and turn over a new page/in the Book of Love.'

If there were a 'Book of Love,' such voices that tell of violence would surely be recorded on its covers.

In the poem she read at the presidential inauguration in Washington, Maya Angelou spoke with lyric intensity of the mixed multitudes of America, the living whose voices and bodies cry out for change. 'Arriving on the nightmare,' the poet dares to hope that they are bought out of mental and physical slavery: their 'passages have been paid.' On the inside back page of the newspaper that carried the text of Angelou's poem, I read of Iraqi children dying from spent shells spat out by American missiles. The spirit of Angelou's fierce compassion forces me back into the desolation of the actual—radioactive shells mimicking nature, contortion that the innocence of childhood could never decipher. Children dying now of the games they played in a war ravaged land, who will pay their passages?

Desert Rose

All the seven skies
are broken
a bright wind seals
the infant's mouth

Sand dunes reap
the pillaged city
the vine bears
fruit

Colossal grapes
of rock
black rock
to have

Or hold
at heart
the driven self
near sightless

As hands
split bread
and strip
the desert rose.

Estrangement Becomes the Mark of the Eagle

I.

We lie in a white room, on a bed with many pillows
next to a window just above a street

You whisper: exile is hard
let me into your mouth, let me blossom

I listen for I know the desert is all around
the muggers and looters, caravan men with masked faces
and Mesopotamia's largesse under tanks
and the colonels of Texas and Florida
with cockatoo feathers in their caps
and the young lads of Oregon torn from their pillows
bent under bombs, grenades, gas masks
and the young lads of Kuwait beheaded in the sand.

II.

Estrangement becomes the mark of the eagle
a signal corpus, bonanza of dew
the portals of paradise are sunk

Yet all that surrenders as we do, lover infant godhead,
nothing makes blank, nothing kills, not
the chill hauteur of elegies, not gunshot wounds

But vision clamps. Bloodied feathers
in a young woman's mouth, torn from a colonel's cap,
she spits them out, she comes from Tiruvella, my hometown
heart undercover, belly huge in desert sand she squats
by the barbed wire of a transit camp outside Amman

Behind her back a ziggurat of neon
marking the eagle's pure ascent
in whose aftermath small bodies puff with ash.

III.

We lie in a white room, on a bed with many pillows
just above the street, the world's a blackened marketplace

No codicil: *Mujh-se pahli-si mahabbat* …dearest heart
I can no longer repeat the rest of that.*

Where we are a child, her jeans filled with blood
gags on dropped vegetables, half-cooked rice
she picked up as she knelt in the trash.
Below her, smashed subway cars imported from Japan
crumple thirty feet down underneath our gate

---

* Note: The entire line runs: 'Mujh-se pahli-si mahabbat, meri mahbub, na mang.' It
is the first line of the celebrated poem by Faiz Ahmed Faiz and in translation may
be rendered as: 'Beloved, do not ask me for that love again.'

While men well trained to the purchase of power
knot water bottles, burst cans of shaving cream
spent condoms, to the rear ends of jeeps and race
at the crack of dawn, at the bitten end of our century
through Broadway, through narrow desert tracks.

Accidental Markings

In Joseph Conrad's *Heart of Darkness*, Marlow speaks of his childhood fascination with maps, with 'blank spaces' that beckoned him. Later, in adulthood, these spaces, even as they fill with rivers and lakes, dwindle into areas of 'darkness.' But what is an area of darkness for the English man, is the site of ordinary life for those who live there. The scents of the leaves haven't changed nor the colors of the sky.

Yet colonial naming rips apart the density of ordinary knowledge, daily life.

What would it be like to be a woman at the water's edge, in such a 'place of darkness,' crying out at the white men who enter her world, changing it forever? How to understand the terror of a history that has torn away place names, shredding sense so that what she knew as her ordinary world has turned into someone else's darkness? What would it be like for her granddaughter fifty, seventy, a hundred years later to try to take back that tree, that river, that ancestry, and in such naming make the world over again?

It is out of shreds like this, out of muscle, bone, iron shards, slings and shots, the cruelty of a world torn away from our bodily senses, that we start to make up our postcolonial stories, start to pick out places and dates, the flow of rivers, unpack a sense that was submerged, mute ancestral memory.

And so to travel in the mind, through places one has known, is also to scrape back history, reveal the knots, the accidental markings of sense and circumstance that make up our lives. To disclose ordinary lives as they cut against the grand narratives of history, the rubric of desire gritty against the supposed truths we have learnt. Poetry becomes part of this difficult labor, weaving a fabric that can bear the gnarled, tangled threads of our lives. Then, too, to cross a border can be to die a little. And the shock of a new life comes in, tearing up the old skin, old habits of awareness.

I wrote "Great Brown River" in my early years in this country, walking by the side of the Mississippi. I had learnt of that river in childhood, from geography books, a close second to the Nile, I was told, in its length, its grandeur. As I walked over the brown earth, over twisted roots, I saw the empty railroad tracks that connect this North American continent. 'Why do the waves have to be like swords?' a man once asked me after reading the poem. I had no answer then, but now I think, perhaps, it's because they have to cut through into newness. Ancestors crawl out of holes in the earth covered by railroad tracks. Touching them, it might be possible to name the earth again.

Great Brown River

This river without a name
I live by:
a great brown river
flecked with foam
where few birds call.

There are freight cars
tethered to the trees
their metal holds
marked *Burlington Northern*
marked *Milwaukee*.

In the pitch black holes
between the rails,
debris of unnumbered lives,
tin cans, chipped glass
worn car tires,
the body of a dead hawk
its wings clapping
in a dry wind
that jars the river silt
batters the freight cars
till out of the blind holes
ancestors wake:

their flesh is brown
as river water,
sugarcane stubble,

iron bits, cut cord
laced to their skin.

Arms braced
they prevent me
from the musical gardens
of the rich,
well-lit fountains,
signs swaying above
this city

like a child's
cut outs:
Best Flour Pilsbury,
Satin Smooth Tips,
Buy Life Insurance.

As they swarm into water
dragging the railroads behind,
I realize this river
will round the earth,
a whole globe seething
with words.
The waves are swords.

Our journeys draw us out into time to come. They force us into the specific densities of our lives, the channels of art. Some of my long poem, "The Storm," came to me in a cold shopping mall in upstate New York. I recall the back of the car loaded with plastic shopping bags, milk, cereal, broccoli, peppers, the cold asphalt all around, the grey sky. I tried to make notes in the car as we circled the parking lot, trying to edge out. The notes turned into stanzas of the poem.

"The Storm: A Poem in Five Parts" marks a journey. It opens by evoking my paternal grandfather who tore down his ancestral house, teak and bronze, centuries old. He tore it down to build a house complete with running water and electricity. To furnish the new house, he used furniture he had once bought from the British Resident.

The poem turns to the difficult passage of migration. Kerala is a place of migrancy. It is as Ireland was in the earlier years of the century. Almost everyone has a relative abroad, in the Gulf or in America.

I wrote a little prefatory note to "The Storm":

"I think of this poem as if it were a folded fan, the kind we used to make as children in the long, stuffy days of the premonsoon season, waiting for the rains to come, chasing away the low, hanging air as best we could. Or as one of the stiff palmyra fans grandmother had hung to the wall. The severe, formal folds in the fan meant that at any one point you only saw several bits of the surface and those, too, only for an instant, as any one part fell into its fragmentary concatenation. As the woman or child moved her hand, the fan shifted, too. And whether it was tugged from the ceiling or wall by an adult, or held in a small child's palm, the function of that fan was motion."

Words, of course, can't work entirely like that, but I do think of "The Storm" as a bits-and-pieces narrative, the only sort my life can fall into. The order of the parts, instead of recovering any hierarchical unity, quiver and replace in the acts of reading. Displacement, violence, but also the poise of a ritualized order are all parts of the feminine world. Nor would I wish to exclude the crudity of supermarkets and airports, the ashen stuff that clings to the imagination and must be washed off.

The Storm: A Poem in Five Parts

I. After the First House

Father's father tore it down
heaped rosewood in pits
as if it were a burial

bore bits of teak
and polished bronze
icons and ancient granary;

the rice grains clung
to each other
soldered in sorrow,

syllables
on grandmother's tongue
as she knelt.

She caught the stalks
in open palms
bleached ends
knotted in silk

cut from the walls
the stained
and whittled parts of fans

that cooled her cheeks
in the aftermath of childbirth

in the hot seasons of the soul
when even the silver boxes
she kept her brocades in
seemed to catch fire and burn.

. . . .

Through thorn and freckled vine
I clambered uphill
following the fragments
of the first house

When I stopped
at a stone upturned
or split mango bark
swarming with ants

I glimpsed the bluish sky
flashing in places

as if the masts
of a great ship wrecked
had pierced it through,

the sun glittering in bare spots
the voices of family
all near and dear
crying from the holds.

The ancestral hillside
the long gardens of our dead
across the swollen paddy fields

moved as if with a life
utterly beyond recall

a power of motion
a fluent, fluid thing
that slipped and struck
against my childish fears
and turned me then all muddy
and green and fearful
into a child who shivered in broad heat,
sensing her flesh as sheer fall:

the cliffs of chalk
hanging by the river,
the pungent depths of waterholes
where buffaloes crawled
light invisible in the well
at the very base,
blade and fractured eggshell
revolving in tense silence.

. . . .

In noonday heat
as pigeons massed the eaves
and the rooster bit
into a speckled hen beneath
I slid the iron bolt.
I crept from the house
on the hill,
its pillars washed in white
walls wired with electricity.
I slid down a slope
all chalky and bruised:
gooseberries ripped themselves loose,
vine scrawled on my thighs

freckled black and bloodied.

In ravines cut by rainfall
in patches where cloves
were dug out in clumps
and the ground let stand
I saw wild ants
mating in heaps.

Acres of sweet grass
thrashed by the heat
scored back,
refused to grow
in the burnt and blackened space
where the first house stood.

▪ ▪ ▪ ▪

Night after night
on pillows hemmed in silk
stitched with rows
of wild flowers

I dreamt of bits and pieces
of the ruined house:
rosewood slit and furrowed
turning in soil,
teak, struck from the alcoves
where the icons hung
bent into waves,

blackened vessels
filled with water
from the disused well

a child's toy
two wheels of tin on a stick
swirling

as if at midnight
the hidden sun
had cast itself down
amidst us,
the golden aura whirling

and voices of beings
who might as well be angels
crying: 'Ai

'Ai Ai
Ai Ai Ai
Not I, Not I'

Meaningless thunder,
lightning from what one presumed
to be the abode of the gods
shaking us to our knees.

. . . .

Through sugarcane stalks
thick and bawdy red
the graves are visible:

grandparents end to end
great uncles and great aunts
cousins dead of brain fever

bald sisters sunk into rage
their brothers-in-law
without issue

ancestors all,
savage, sinless now,
their stones stung white with rain.

I peer from the rubble
where a first house stood,
the centuries swarm through me.

A king crawls out
on his hands and knees
he stamps his foot
he smashes the golden bull
that held him whole

'Come catch me now'
he sings
'Look at me
I am born again!'

He leaps
through mud and sugar
cane stalks,
squats low and bares himself.

Through monsoon clouds
waves dip and crown
his blunt head.

. . . .

Neither king nor clown
I am hurt
by these tales
of resurrection.

I can count
the grey hairs
on my head,
heavy lines
on my palm
natural occurrences
I cannot command,
cannot dispel

casting art
to the edge
of an old wooden theater

where I wait
in the wings
with the two-bit actresses
the old man
who fumbles for his wig,
the eunuch
adjusting the hem of his sari.

Rouge burns
on his cheek
as he watches
the young lad
rock feverishly
on a wooden horse.

II. The Travellers

A child thrusts back a plastic seat
rubs her nose against glass,
stares hard as jets strike air,
the tiny men in their flying caps
with bright gold braid
invisible behind the silver nose.

Is there no almanac
for those who travel ceaselessly?
No map where the stars
inch on in their iron dance?

The gulls that swarm
on the sodden rocks
of the Red Sea, the Gulf of Aqaba
cry out to us in indecipherable tongues,
the rough music of their wings
torments us still.

Tears stream down the cheeks
of the child voyager,
from the hot tight eyes.
The mother combing out her hair
behind a bathroom door
tugging free a coiled hem,
cannot see her eldest daughter.

A mile or two away
in an ancient square
guns cough and stutter

Through acres of barbed wire
shutting off shops
and broken parlors

they bear the bodies of the dead

Pile them in lorries
and let the mothers
in their blackened veils approach.

Some collapse
on the steep slope of grief
crawl on hands and knees,
piteous supplication of the damned.

Others race to tear
the bloodstained cloth
gaze at the stiffened brow
and shattered jaw
parts without price
precious sediments of love.

In Baghdad's market places
in the side streets of Teheran,
in Beirut and Jerusalem
in Khartoum and Cairo,
in Colombo and New Delhi,
Jaffna, Ahmedabad and Meerut
on the highways of Haryana
in poorly lit cafes
to the blare of transistors
in shaded courtyards
where children lisp
we mourn our dead

Heaping leaves and flowers
that blossom only in memory
and the red earth
of this mother country
with its wells and watering places

onto countless graves.

.   .   .   .

I sometimes think that in this generation
there is no more violence than there ever was,
no more cruelty, no greater damnation.

We have hung up white flags
in refugee camps, on clothes lines
strung through tenements,
on the terraces of high walled houses.

Peering through my window at dawn
I see the bleached exhausted faces,
men and women knee deep in mud in the paddy beds,
others squatting by the main road to the sea
break granite with blunt hammers

Sickles are stacked
by the growing pile of flint,
the hammers draw blood.

Children scrabble in the dirt
by the hovels of the poor.
In monsoon rain they scrawl
mud on their thighs,
their lips are filled with rain.

I see movie theaters built with black
money from the Gulf,
air-conditioned nightmares
bought for a rupee or two,
the sweaty faces of the rich
the unkempt faces of the struggling middle class.

Next door in a restaurant
food is served on white cloth
and the remnant flung to the crows.

Let me sing my song
even the crude parts of it,
the decrepit seethe of war,
cruelty inflicted in clear thought,
thought allied to brutal profiteering
the infant's eyes still filled with sores.

. . . .

Consider us crawling forward
in thunder and rain,
possessions strewn through airports
in dusty capitals,
small stoppages in unknown places
where the soul sleeps:

Bahrain, Dubai, London, New York,
names thicken and crack
as fate is cut and chopped
into boarding passes.

German shepherds sniff our clothes
for the blind hazard of bombs,
plastique knotted into bras,
grenades stuffed into a child's undershirt.

Our eyes dilate
in the grey light of cities
that hold no common speech for us,
no bread, no bowl, no leavening.

At day's close we cluster
amidst the nylon and acrylic
in a wilderness of canned goods,

aisles of piped music
where the soul sweats blood:

Migrant workers stripped
of mop and dirty bucket,
young mothers who scrub kitchen floors
in high windowed houses
with immaculate carpets,

Pharmaceutical salesmen in shiny suits
night nurses raising their dowry
dollar by slow dollar
tired chowkidars eking their pennies out
in a cold country

Students, aging scholars,
doctors wedded to insurance slips,
lawyers shoveling their guilt
behind satin wallpaper.

Who can spell out
the supreme ceremony
of tea tins
wedged
under the frozen food counter?

Racks of cheap magazines
at the line's end
packed with stars

Predict our common birth
yet leave us empty handed
shuffling damp bills.

. . . .

A child stirs in her seat
loosens her knees,
her sides shift
in the lap of sleep

the realm of dream
repairs

as if a woman
glimpsed through a doorway
whose name is never voiced

took green silk
in her palms

threaded it
to a sharp needle,
drew the pleats together:

a simple motion
filled with grace,
rhythmic repetition
in a time of torment.

In the child's dream
the mother seated
in her misty chair
high above water,
rocks her to sleep
then fades away.

The burning air
repeats her song,
gulls spin and thrash
against a stormy rock

rifts of water
picket light,
a fisherman stumbles
upright

in his catamaran.

That Other Body

The imagination strikes against the stones of a city, against the stubble at the edge of a city.

The stones and stubble cry back.

The response cannot be willed. The will has little to do with the workings of imagination.

I must write what I hear: both cry and response, till the poem, instead of being cut and polished like a stone—though who does not long for solidity, for precision?—is glimpsed as a body, another body, *chinmaya deha*.

This other body is formed within mine, at times with the speed of lightning, at times with the infinite patience of sunlight that strikes at a billowing curtain, muslin puffing and weaving in the wind.

This image has force. It fills my hollow body with light, tilts the exile that is so often forced upon us so that to say 'I,' in another country, becomes a recognition of truth.

Change comes from this voice, this listening: the imagination striking the world, the world crying out in its own innumerable tongues.

'A garden inclosed is my sister, my spouse...'

Out of her window she sees the garden of pheasants. The emperor has been dead for fifteen years. The garden is flooded with British soldiers, many of them young lads. They scoop up potatoes with their bare hands, scrub them, then toss them into the boiling cauldron. The cauldron stands where the bench of the princess stood, by the patch of winter jasmine, in the garden of pheasants.

The soldiers are red faced, raw between the ears with sunlight. They have not stood the long trek from Oudh very well. The dust bites her eyes. She sees one of the soldiers lean over the cauldron. He is stirring the water with a long stick. His face vanishes in the steam.

She turns away into the darkness of the room, rubbing her eyes. Her hands, tired with holding the pen, hurt her. She wonders if the muscles are falling apart. She clenches her fist. Why is she reading the *Song of Solomon* anyway, at high noon, in the middle of writing a history of the emperor?

The words flash in her head: 'garden,' 'enclosed,' 'sister,' 'spouse.' She leans for an instant against the wall, shutting her eyes, opening up her body to the darkness, then strides, pen in hand to her desk. As she lowers herself into the chair, it comes to her slowly, with utter certitude, those words were penned by a woman. Why has the authorship been concealed for thousands of years?

She stares out of the window, gripped by a sudden desolation she cannot name, numb in the fiftieth year of her life with the loneliness that can come from living in a woman's body.

'It is a house, a poverty, my flesh is a history,' she murmurs.

'But it has no dates. I cannot point to it and say, "that," "there," "then," and then I am plunged in it.'

She sees five soldiers stirring the potatoes. Each one of them, born of woman. Why have they come here? She sees them drink at the pitcher of death.

Saraswatiamma, famous author of the *Uprising of Ulloor*, grandmother's contemporary, will never finish her history. She watches the dust rise over the broken trellises of the winter jasmine, the dry grass, the hot pebbles in the garden of pheasants. She sees a child cry, its mouth horribly open, filled with dust.

She knows the body is a house.

New World Aria

I see a city filled with women. No, I must correct that. I see small fires, in garbage cans, by the park benches, twigs smoldering at the edge of doorways shielded by darkness. The fires bristle, then slowly, with a great roaring, rise into the air. The trees by the river glow in the heat and birds hidden in the leaves start to sing.

Driven out by the heat, as if they themselves had not set the flames roaring with cans of kerosene, with tiny matchboxes pilfered from kitchen and restaurant, the women come running. Hundreds, thousands of them, a mountain of women gathered by the river. River water turns rosy with fiery reflections from the flames falling off the tall glass buildings in the downtown part of the city.

Suddenly I hear a sharp voice crying, 'Where are the children?' Then louder, 'Where are the men?' The mountain starts to quiver. Someone lifts up her grey skirts, another her torn black sari. Arms and legs poke out, beards, thighs, hairy chests, tiny quivering lips.

In all that cacophony, as men and children stumble out to safety, I listen to a short woman singing. She cannot sing very well, but her voice helps. In that awkward music, someone passes out bits of bread, no matter that it is hard and moldy. Another pours out milk. Where did she find that old pitcher, milk blue at the rim? A third starts slicing apples, the fruit resting on a stone. A fourth, lean and hungry, her hair tied back with a dark scarf, stares back. 'Yes, yes,' she whispers, 'the old city must burn.'

I think she mutters something about learning how to build, but hidden in the overhanging tree, body drenched with sweat, I lose her words. I shall fall, I think, break arms, legs, split my lips into tiny morsels. I shall be silenced, entirely, or speak in odd, un-intelligible tongues. My mother's eyes—she left me so very many years ago and I was forced to fend for myself by the riverbank, picking up scraps of food, using leaves to wipe my blood, sleeping in trees—flash before me.

Just as I sense I am falling into that fiery darkness, I catch the voices of ten thousand women, no longer strangers to each other, singing.

No Nation Woman

How shall I tell of these travels? How shall I make up my story? My earliest departure from India—there is little in it that could turn into the stuff of epic. I did not leave my motherland because of terror or political repression. I was not torn away from my ancestral home by armed militants. I did not come from a shtetl, a wordless child forced out by marauding Cossacks. On the brink of turning five, I left with my mother on a ship, left behind the radiant love of my grandparental home, quite simply because my father got a job he wanted to take, for a few years, far away in another country. A country in North Africa across an ocean and a sea.

Over the fault lines of my life I have unfurled a resolute picture, a flag that fluttered into a sheet and grew and grew. A simple shining topography. A large house with a red tiled roof and two courtyards, one in which the passion fruit vine spreads its delicate tentacles by the kitchen window, the other in which the mulberry bush my grandmother planted years before my birth stubbornly thrusts its roots into the soil and refuses to die. A house with a garden, a street running by it, a little dusty in the dry season with water buffaloes, a bridge, a white painted church.

But that shining picture has tormented me. Faced with it, my real life has dwindled and diminished. And my words have recoiled back into a vacant space in the mind, a place of waste, dingy detritus of a life uncared for, no images to offer it hospitality. I ask myself, am I a creature with no home, no nation? And if so, what new genus could I possibly be?

Sometimes I have tried to puzzle it out: if I were a man, I might have turned myself into something large and heroic, a creature of quest and adventure, a visionary with power in his grasp. Instead, as a woman, the best I can be is something small and stubborn, delicate perhaps at the best of times, but irrefutably persistent. After all, when has my life gone according to plan? It seems a poor thing to say, but the best I have learnt has to do with unlearning the fixed positionings I was taught, trusting my own nose, diving into the waves, tale telling.

How can tale telling work, when faced with ceaseless water? How shall I sing of Ashtamudi Lake, where the train toppled in, where young girls dressed in white make up an elegy for corpses unshriven, swarming in water?

A few years ago, the train from Bangalore crashed in. No one knows if the bridge caved in or if the driver, exhausted by the night journey, lost control. The villagers near the water were brave. They leapt in, rescuing those they could. As they dived in, their eyes and mouth were covered with filthy water. One man, well past middle age, stooped, eyes shut, into the water. The body he touched, the body he lifted out, was that of his own son.

At first he did not understand. On wild grass he laid down his precious burden. Then he laid himself next to the boy. Stretching out his old man's body, he tried to stop breathing.

The sky was very clear that day, and there were waterlilies by the edge of the water, utterly untouched by bits of metal, human flesh and blood in the lake. Waterlilies the color of sulphur.

The old man shut his eyes. He covered his nose and mouth with his hands and tried to stop breathing. Breath exploded out. Next to him lay the waterlogged body of his son. With one hand, he touched the tangled hair. A crashing sound in the sky, he heard it in his inmost ear. He thought he was dead already, that he held his infant son in his arms again, in the darkness of a small hut by the water's edge, at the very hour of the child's birth.

. . . .

When I was a child, when it came time each year to leave Tiruvella and return to Khartoum, I used to try and stop my breath. Pinch my nostrils, tamp up my mouth with a fist. But I could never manage it for long and, as my head filled with blood, the breath burst outwards.

Using that breath I raced to my hiding place, down by the railway line where pink stalks of tapioca grew taller than a six year child. Like a kurianna I crouched, bottom up, trying to bury my face in the soil. The taste of black earth was on my tongue, sharp scent of tapioca root, raw, hidden. I needed to go on breathing though. With the breath coming and going, going and coming, I tried not to breathe in dirt.

Tale telling is like breathing. If you try to hold it in, it explodes outwards. Sometimes in my effort to stop I would think of what it would be like to turn into a stone or a rock in the front garden in Tiruvella. But what would that solve? If I were a stone, amma could so easily pick me up—and surely she would. Surely she would come crying into her father's garden, under stalks of jasmine and mulberry, stand there. Or stand in the wild grass, crying, where is my child, my first child, my Meena? Surely she would come and, catching sight of my half-buried form, the two-inch stone with reddish streaks I had turned into, grab hold of me, tuck me into her black handbag, the one appa brought her from Beirut.

Tucking me into her bag, she would make off in great haste, leaping into a metal body that traveled at great speed, over crossroads, boundaries of nations, oceans, cutting from house to house, state to state, never stopping, never resting, my stony self bound always in her bag, held in a metallic thing with wheels, wings coasting or steam puffing as we moved over earth, sky, water.

So what would it have been like to be, before all motion was, before the first hiccuping breath, before the first sky? Before train, plane, ship, exile?

. . . .

Houses shatter and fall in me. Shards of them, bits and pieces of them, a room with a wall all askew, a kitchen with a side door blown off so the sun shines in, a bit of a threshold, part of a high latticed window, teak steps as high as a grown man, bits of sand and gravel someone's foot brought in.

When I try to look back at my life there's no backness to it. It's all around, a moistness like sweet well water, the houses crumbled up inside. How many houses have there been? When I count it sears me: a hot wind that destroys generations. Makes history a mad, mad joke. Let me try to count it out in all the numbers I know, even if I sound like a three year old.

Numbers tumble in the spray of sound: *Aune, runde, mune, nale. Eak, do theen char.* One, two, three, four. *Wahid, ithneen, thalatha arba. Un deux trois quatre.* I have used up all my languages. I have only got as far as four. But there were many more houses. Were there four times four? More than that, too. The forest of numbers makes no sense.

I try to lay it all out on a cloth, an imaginary cloth, but it turns uneven, stained, fit to shred with the pressure exerted on it. The houses grow tipsy.

Houses to be born in, houses to die in, houses to make love in with wet, sticky sheets, houses with the pallor of dove's wings, houses fragrant as cloves and cinammon ground together. Ah, the thickness of the tongue that will not let me be, will not let me lay it out, saying: I was born here, I lived here, I did this, I did that, saying it all out in the way that people do or like to do.

Houses in Allahabad, in Pune, then southwards through the Nilgiris and the curved rock face of the Palghat Pass, the ancestral houses in Tiruvella and Kozhencheri—houses of blood and bone where I have lived and died in countless lives before mine. In an old steamer painted white, westwards over the Indian Ocean, through Port Sudan with the waters stained maroon by hidden corals, by train through the desert till we reach the houses in Hai-el-Matar, in Khartoum. There were acacia trees and the fierce water of the Blue Nile that drew in unsuspecting swimmers, gunfire in the market place, tear gas. I carried the acid scent with me over the Atlantic, eighteen, shivering in my thin clothes as the plane touched down.

I live in England, in a tall house on Oxford Street, in Nottingham, Lawrence country. I have a dormer window, I paint, love riotously, write a thesis on memory. It makes me mad, writing that thesis, all about reclaiming time. While the mind cuts loose from the body and circles empty space. Small spells in Galway, in Amsterdam, in Chinon where the Loire pours through rocks. In Nottingham, I lean out of the window. Where is blood hidden here? In the cherry trees?

I return to the Palghat Pass, the rock face harder now, echoing my cries: 'I am I, woman of innumerate houses.' Entering the old courtyard, I become mute. I roll myself in reams and reams of paper and wait in the dry houses of Pune, Delhi, Hyderabad.

All shit and paper now, I have no eyes, no face.

There, there, I must stop myself, I can't.

This housekeeping exercise isn't getting anywhere. And what to do with the rest of life?

Houses in America, the little rooms painted white, the parquet floors, the rush basket I set on fire in Minneapolis with a smoldering cigarette. What to do with the trucks that rumble under the windows at 242nd Street and Broadway in the great city of Manhattan where the air is never clean? Trucks rolling by Poe Cottage in the Bronx, where Edgar Allan Poe moved for the clearer air. Now the air is filthier than where he was, the bars burnt out, the street covered with potholes. They managed to set his little cottage on a piece of parkland, put chain fences around it, install a lecturer from City College who gives visitors a little speech on electricity, how Poe was struck, what lightning did to him.

But what is Poe to me? I have not been to his tombeau. What do I know of women called Annabelle Lee? What does he know of me, I might ask? My house is split through, a fault in the ground where it stands. They're auctioning my soul where they auction fish, catfish, swordfish, scooped from the Arabian sea, ten thousand miles from Poe's cottage by the old wharf, by the paddy beds on the Tiruvella-Kozhencheri Road.

Thinking of the old road calms me. It runs between the two houses that have always been there for me, the Tiruvella and Kozhencheri houses, different as idli from dosa, plum pudding from peach pie, akin nonetheless, with tiled roofs, cool floors, windows cut in teak, polished brass latches, no glass there.

I am at home on the road that bumps a little as it passes the old wharf, where at dawn the fishermen crowd, laying out their wares, crying out the prices of shrimp, catfish, swordfish, parrotfish, sardines, soles, hot, houseless soles dredged from the mothering sea.

White Horseman Blues

'For what is the present after all but a growth out of the past?/(As a projectile formed, impell'd, passing a certain line, still keeps on...)'

—Walt Whitman, "Passage to India"

I.

'People come to America to forget,' he said, rubbing his chin. 'Surely you see that?'

She gazed at him. Outside the street was filled with cars.

'Here,' he said, 'tell me what you're xeroxing, and why?'

'A poem,' she murmured.

'Why that?' He pointed at the pages of the book.

'Bobrowski's poem,' she answered. 'It's called, "Dead Language."'

No sooner were the words out of her mouth than she saw another behind him, neck askew. She noticed the heavy object this other held was a head, his own head. Out of the mouth, and out of holes for the eyes, came smoke.

'Why is he here?' she whispered, pointing.

II.

As if the root were cleft, double arching darkness split and furrowed in soil, moist, distinct particles both fed and hurt, the voice making itself up, all over again. The language essential as moisture to the driving root, sap to the stalk, flesh to the succulent shoot, is split, over and over again: vowels stripped, syllables skinned. No beginning, no ending there. The bough is always snapping, the rockaby baby tumbling through air.

Tumbling through air, air ablaze, petticoats trailing wisps of smoke.

The white man on a horse races through Queen Victoria's palace. He shakes his whip in his hand. He cannot tolerate the noise in his head. He craves silence, total silence. The natives are to be raised, their condition ameliorated.

The horse snorts at the mirrors borne over from India, mica edged with platinum, etched in the patterns of mango leaf and jasmine. The mirrors take badly to the dampness in the palace. The horse races through the mirror on the right. The horseman loses his head. 'Umph, umph, there, there,' he gulps.

He is on the point of choking, a body, headless, that must see itself seeing.

The maps are blank, white. The place-names swarm like maggots.

III.

How did I learn this language?

I was a plump, dark child. Ugly, cast out, scrounging for words in the tapioca patch, at the edge of the dinner table. Gobbling up words like the old turkey with its scarlet wattles. Watching the white horse race on the dusty road toward the church. Watching the horseman without a head as he was led out of the church.

He holds out his head to me.

The shores of America come closer, the Rocky Mountains, the clefts filled with mica and igneous rock, Colorado canyons, deserts of Arizona and New Mexico, shorelines of Manhattan island, Brooklyn Bridge, rocking on its cords of steel, fit for a new birth, fit for the thousands of cars, trucks, bicycles, pedestrians.

I slip off my chappals, cross the bridge on bare feet.

Metal burns. Ahead of me is the horseman. Dismounting from his horse he leads the way. His hands are smoking. He holds his head, gingerly.

When we pass the Watchtower, with its neon sign—'The End of the World is at Hand'—he hiccups.

IV.

The syllables on the other side of the bridge, by the building of the Jehovah's Witnesses, are swathed in smoke. There is smoke in my mouth, my eyes.

This is my autobiography.

When the infant falls out of the crib (the crib sheets are raised, the mother weeps in her clothing, fully dressed, ready for the wedding), the girl child shivers in her thin dress.

One of her front teeth, fragile as pearl, is slipping out. Her lips are plum colored, too wide apart for modesty.

She is falling now, with the tiny infant, with the old woman already floating in water. The child's skirts float up, revealing her thighs and the soft, succulent warmth of her inner flesh.

Her skirts are burning.

Perhaps the wind will put out the flames, cool the syllables.

V.

She walks over the bridge. She is so close behind the horseman, she can almost touch him. His back grows shadowy, she can hardly see the stump of his neck for all that vapor. Exhaust fumes, from cars fixed to the tracks.

The bridge rocks under her. Waves glitter, glass on the xerox machine.

Light darts around her face. She sees her face in the black waters of the East River, spoked with light.

'I am memory!' she cries out loud. She puts out her hands to the water. Her feet, as she walks to the other side, are steady and cool.

The cars glint tinier than ants, molten, held to their tracks.

Has the horseman tossed his head into the East River?

A streak of pearl, a sudden fizzle, then something that looks very like a pith helmet floats under the keel of a passing boat.

Waves mass, whiter than pages torn from a book.

Whose book? As she crosses the bridge, she sees lines she can write in a flowing script.

Tongues of the new world blazing.

Migrant Music

'In order to belong you need a past.'

I look out the window at the river flecked with mist, the squat houses of New Jersey I cannot see beyond.

'The struggle for sense is compact with the struggle for a past.'

He said all this to me, a man whose name I cannot reveal.

His hands were shaped like an instrument.

'Can you play this?' he asked, before the mist took him away.

The past: a stringed instrument I must play, inventing what I need—a crude thing pieced together with chair caning, wood from a mirror's frame, a clay bowl holding a few dried roots.

Across the river, the cliffs turn, bony, irresolute, the houses blank.

Even the trees are like pious little girls, veiled in mist.

I see my father's father, two-decades dead, head bald, fists bristling with banyan roots.

Legs astride the cliffs of New Jersey, muscles squat and monstrous, he is drenched in sweat:

I hear him call. He is calling my name.

A Durable Past

How can I make a durable past in art, a past that is not merely nostalgic, but stands in vibrant relation to the present? This is the question that haunts me.

It forces me back into a present forged through multiple anchorages.

Sometime back, I wrote a few lines as a reflection on what it means to be a writer here. This is what I wrote and I'll read it out:

'As much as anything, I am a poet writing in America. But American poet? What sort? Surely not of the Robert Frost or Wallace Stevens variety. An Asian-American poet then? Clearly that sounds better. But poet tout court. Just poet. Will it fit? Not at all. There is very little that I can be tout court in America. Except perhaps woman, mother. But even there I wonder.

'Everything that comes to me is hyphenated: a woman-poet, a woman-poet-of-color, a South-Indian-woman-poet who makes up lines in English, a postcolonial language, as she waits for the red lights to change on Broadway, a Third-World-woman-poet, who takes as her right the inner city of Manhattan, making up poems about the hellhole of the subway line, the burnt-out blocks so close to home on the Upper West Side.

'O confusions of the heart, thicknesses of the soul, the borders we cross tattooing us all over! Is there any here beyond this skin-flicking thing where we can breathe and sing? Yet our song must also be a politics, a perilous thing, crying out for a place where the head is held high in sunlight, so that one is not merely a walking wound, a demilitarized zone, a raw sodden trench.'

'I am thinking now of lines from Frantz Fanon, who speaks of the dividing line, the barracks, the barbed wire that exists in a colonized state. What he says is applicable to Asian-American art. He speaks of that 'zone of occult instability' we must come to in our art, in our culture of decolonization. I use the word 'decolonization' advisedly because we bear within us histories that are not visible to the world around. For us, here, the barbed wire is taken into the heart and art grapples with a disorder in society. In our writing, we need to evoke a chaos coequal to the injustices that surround us.'

. . . .

But where identity is concerned, this can result in a curious sense of unselving. It is from this consciousness of unselving that I create my work. And so there is a subtle violence for me involved in the production of the work, even as this labor of writing is one of the most intimate things I do as a person.

And this awareness, even in its very difficulty, is a part of our historical moment. And perhaps this awareness can keep us wary, lest in the creation of a new, emergent art, almost without knowing it, we are bought and sold, our images magnified in the high places of capitalist chic. And so we make works which, even as they take their place in the social world, are recalcitrant to it. For these works, born in privacy, must enter the public space, rupture it, rework community.

In our multiple ethnicities as Asian Americans, we are constantly making alliances, both within and outside our many communities. In order to make up my ethnic identity as an Indian American, I learn from Japanese Americans, Korean Americans, Chinese Americans, African Americans, Native Americans, Hispanic Americans, Jewish Americans, Arab Americans. And these images that slip and slide out of my own mind jostle against a larger, shared truth. And my artwork refracts these lines of sense, these multiple anchorages.

And such lateral holdings take the place that a tradition might in a more continuous art form. And perhaps this is precisely what writing in America gives me: a rich, vivid sense of space, a welter of experience that cannot be easily held together in a single language. And only through acknowledging this shifting, coruscating present can I create a durable past in art. I think of Walt Whitman's meditations on the organic form he envisaged: 'From the eyesight proceeds another eyesight and from the hearing proceeds another hearing and from the voice proceeds another voice eternally curious of the harmony of things with man.'

Performing the Word

We are gathered here to celebrate the written word, upright, rejoicing. And behind the word, our shared lives, for the word is always human, spoken out of mouths, written by our hands, forged by the living body.

We inhabit a world divided into bits and pieces, locked into nations, cultures, languages, creeds, distinct and multifarious. Through this we find our livelihood as writers. We struggle to make sense, overcome unnatural distinctions. To try and reduce our world to homogeneity spawns terror, 'terrifying singularity,' Salman Rushdie called it. Making it all one is to subjugate, shred up, destroy.

What does it mean to kill a writer? To prevent, stop up his or her speech, censor, shred, ban. It also implies the literal from which we try to avert our eyes: kill, maim, destroy the living body. Those who have called for the murder of Rushdie have now said: 'It might be enough if all copies of his book are burnt, destroyed the world over.' The book is an icon of the body and his book is in this world of exploding margins, cacophonous play he celebrates. But the world is at the same time the chaos that swallows up all fictions. Third World writers know this. The Indian subcontinent has known colonialism, the violence of Partition, the fury of communal warfare.

I think of Safdar Hashmi, a young playwright and actor, born like Rushdie into a Muslim family in India, seven years younger though. On a clear winter's day in Ghaziabad, just north of Delhi, not yet thirty-five years old, Hashmi was beaten to death. He was killed as he was performing. It was on January 1, the first day of this new year. The next day in Ram Manohar Lohia hospital, he died of his wounds. Blows had been quite deliberately aimed at his head with the intent to kill.

Safdar was a brave man. He waited in the courtyard, holding the rickety iron gate shut while his fellow performers scaled the walls to safety. His glasses had been smashed in the attack. He could hardly see. In a self-portrait he sketched, one sees the harsh lines of the pencil filling in the face, swift strokes over the neck, curved lines for the hair. But where the eyes should be are squares of white, two gazing straight at the visible world, utterly unflinching. I think Hashmi knew what the cost was, of his life, his art.

Politically, he was a man of progressive sympathies, a member of the CPI(M), involved in the cause of oppressed, underpaid workers, active, too, in women's causes. Among his works of street theater performed by the Jan Natya Manch is *Aurat* (Woman) first performed in 1979. He wrote the lyrics and helped make the script for the Mediastorm video about the Roop Kanwar sati, an event glorified by Hindu extremists.

Why was Hashmi killed? He was an actor killed performing in the street, a writer murdered uttering his words. They were frightened of his words. It was a political act, this murder of a gifted man. He was performing in support of a seven-day industrial strike. Two plays were performed in the impoverished working-class district where he was murdered, Jhandapur, the site of his action, his death. The first of these, *ChakkaJam* (Jammed Wheel), depicted workers who were paid so badly they could hardly survive. The real life of the people on strike was imaged back for them. The second play, *Halla Bol* (Attack), was a sequel. Local elections to the Ghaziabad municipality were coming up. The CPI(M) was strengthening its base among the migrant workers from the countryside who formed a large part of the electorate there. The plays performed by the theater group crystallized the fears, the aspirations of the workers. Roughly a hundred and fifty armed goondas, paid thugs, supporters of the Congress (I) candidate, a member of the ruling party, broke up the performance, scattered the players, hunted down Hashmi and killed him. They also shot to death a twenty-two-year-old factory worker, Ram Bahadhur.

On January 4, three days after his death, the players, led by Safdar's wife, the actress Moloyashree, returned to Jhandapur to the very street where they were performing during the attack. It was a passion play, in the clear winter air just north of Delhi. The sunlight hot, stark. The players dressed in black. They finished the interrupted play.

Those who are free to live and move and speak, do so. As we do now, in front of the United Nations, in fine spring weather. Our voices will not be reduced by terror. We are poets and writers. We will persist. We will sing through our words our very right to speak. This is a testament.*

---

* Note: "Performing the Word" is based on a statement read at the Dag Hammarskjold Plaza, United Nations, New York as part of the PEN Freedom to Write meeting, March 15, 1989.

For Safdar Hashmi Beaten to Death Just Outside Delhi

Safdar it is done:

A courtyard with four walls
where the lock did not hold
a faulty pump, water trickling
out of sight

A winter's day in Jhandapur
under these leaves
wet with light
death a player hundred armed

Clubbed and ringed:
how tight you held the door
so others might race
over wall and stony field

I hear you now knocking
at my door seeking entry.
This room is framed by trees
stones, walls, bare sky

So blue it might be Delhi
in winter all over again

and by the open window
your half-finished play

The actors drenched
in black repeating it
to stubborn stones
children crouched by walls

Grown men and women
packed by the factory walls
and in the distance
the hodgepodge of state

Trucks, tanks, a convoy
of arms irregular, ill-sorted
with boy soldiers, hundred
headed, breathing hard.

Moloyashree

Moloyashree
you come to me in fine weather—

An old mattress with pinpricks
in it puffs cotton;
I see stones and sticks
a child skips over
a woman beats a pan
scraping out burnt milk
stoops behind a torn curtain
crying, 'Ram, Sri Ram, Ram'
crickets flash in mounds of wheat.

Already the sun's in your teeth
the bizarre ivory it turns of a Delhi winter
so fierce it stings cloth and hair.

There
there they beat him by the tap
on scalp and skull with bits of rock
lathis tipped with steel, wrought iron
broken from the construction site.

You point out the spot, so silently
drawing your palms apart as if your
soul and his still hung on a thread

So hot only the dead could work
that needle, crawl through its eye.

Making up Memory

Reflections of a Writer in New York City

For many years now, I have lived in Manhattan. The city fronts me. It is here that I must make up memory, a memory co-equal to the tensions of a city filled with immigrants. The scents, the stench of migrancy is everywhere in Manhattan, in the small shop fronts, on the sidewalks spilling with vegetables, fish caught from the Hudson, sold in the dark alleyways, drying in the burnt-out houses, just a block away.

Sometimes I hear voices, voices of beings, hovering outside a window as a parrot might or on the tip of the candle flame as the candle burns on the windowsill. Imagined beings haunt me, a bird with green feathers filling the winter window.

A bird in a bush

Cried out to her
in a tongue no one
had ever foretold

A green bird
with red flecks in its wings
metal in its beak

'Cuchucuchu bird!'
 She put out her wrist

felt a sharp peck.

As the beak drew blood
she quivered into two:
sun and moon of memory

Coupling in indigo.
The bush turned ivory
and the cold wind blew.

The wind beats against the glass, there is the shriek of ambulances, police cars racing on Riverside Drive. Black waters of the Hudson shining, water lights reflected from New Jersey, fragile, poised like torn petals.

Next morning the snow starts to fall, on river water. I think back to the Pamba, the river of my childhood in Kerala, the Nile, the river of my girlhood in Khartoum. Rivers of Asia, rivers of Africa, memory flowing through harsh rock, muddy borders, the delicate sapphire of the waterlilies lit by sun.

The snow thickens. The parrot in Banabhatta's *Kadambari* caught in a cage. The king questions the parrot, the parrot questions me:

'Tell me everything about yourself, starting with your birth. Where were you born? Who gave you your name? Who is your mother? Who is your father? Do you remember what happened to you in another life?...How were you caught in this cage?'

Am I caught in a cage? Discrete metal bars, panes of glass, all part of brute, physical reality. But the cage must be lowered into the grid of city blocks, sense shattered into multifoliate form, so that over and against nostalgias that would have me say, 'Rivers of Asia, Rivers of Africa,' I can start to remember. Start to make up memory.

The city fronts me. I cannot escape the city. It is here I must remember. A female remembering, the body voiced against the shocking white of silence, against the flames another woman was thrown into, in the city of Hyderabad, where I once lived. That woman's sari set on fire with kerosene because she did not bring in enough dowry. Because a woman is nothing who cannot bring in money, property, new manhood.

A city where women were raped in the communal riots, their veils shredded, mouths stuffed with stones.

Brief Chronicle by Candlelight

Children torn by the winds
married women burnt in their own homes
I thought I had seen it all that night
as I lit a candle at my door.

In the brief chronicle of candlelight
I cried out as a child might
to all the night creatures I know:
jackal, cobra, the thousand-eyed owl.

I thought the wind howled in the badam tree.
In a forest of bamboo once bent to a storm
I heard hundreds of whispering feet.
Countless women, their hours lent

to pounding grain
massaging the ankles of strangers,
their necks spent with bearing bricks
sticks, straw for fires that could one day consume them

would they perish at the muddy center
of all our gathered lives?
I tell you I watched them that night.

Very simply they set their feet
to the waiting trees and climbed them.

They wandered in the night sky
telling the stars in wonder

wrapping us, for we were cold that night
in a true story

a benediction that called up the cobra
from its hole under the stones:
it danced on its tail
in a future light

the jackal pranced by the ancient stones
delighting the sleepy children,
like a raw creature the owl cried out
'tweet-t-woot' and all its thousand eyes
could not drink up the moving women.

In my city apartment, I lean against the windowsill. To the left of the river are the columns of Grant's Tomb, the cupola raised above the trees on the slight mound. There is snow on the hill, snow on the trees, snow swirling in the sky all about the tomb. Snow boiling off the rooftops below me.

Translating that snow into the white space of the page, I make up a poem, an irregular sonnet. But the very act of writing is haunted by the fact that I never knew snow as a child, never experienced cold like this, never saw the sky swirl with bits of whiteness.

'I never knew snow as a child. I cannot remember snow. So how can I continue to write here?' I put these words down on a piece of paper, fold the paper into tiny squares, set the slender thickness in a dark drawer. Something works in that darkness.

The gash in imagined time becomes quite precisely the place memory works itself out. A migrant memory, a memory in flight, yet bound forever to the subtle senses of the body.

And through this memory works a voice.

No, not mine, rather the voice that works through me, a speech inscribed midway between terror—the tyranny of state, the wheel of worlds into which a female body is cast—and the tenderness of elegy. But it is here that desire turns, in the fluidity of this speech, illumining ruptured time.

I cannot forget this city that lies all around. Around and inside me, an intoxicant releasing memory. There's an odd fit for me here, something in the way space works with remembrance, letting loose these breakable rhythms, rhythms of breath, rhythms of meaning, rhythms of bodily sense cut from continuity, redisposed in the dense living spaces of a metropolis.

I think of memory sliced up in slabs, remade, inventing what was lost. City blocks chopping up memory, the subway tearing through it, speed releasing the amnesiac bolt that locks in so much of life spent in multiple places.

The questions that come with dislocation are not necessarily new: Where am I? Who am I? and hardest of all, When am I?

 But the forms of invention these questions propose to a postcolonial consciousness—a life reworked through the seams of a language that is mine and not mine, clothing, forms of life that all retain the bite of old oppressions as well as the pungency of newness—require shining topologies still to be worked out.

The hellhole of the city turned angelic.

I will live here. At the edges of danger, memory flares up.

In India, as a young woman, I read Ralph Waldo Emerson. I was fascinated by the notion of a ceaseless present. What might it mean to have a self that was 'free' of time? That could blossom in individuality? After all, India, like America, is one of the world's most populous democracies. Yet as a woman growing up, so much of what came to me was through the requirements of femininity, the culture and ceremony that sanctified, the strict cast desire was forced to take. The burden of the past seemed insuperable. Might it be possible to cross a border and be free? Freedom for what? To make up a self, the great dream of the possible worlds?

Arriving in America I sensed with something akin to a moral shock that any self I had would be insuperably marked as Indian; that the ethereal freedom was a thing of the head; that the body and heart were Other. The blank space I had conceived of, indeed, was an emptiness, emptiness underwritten with iron.

I mused on the Papal Bull that Christopher Columbus had received from the Pope in his voyages to what he thought was India: the absolute writ to territory. And this musing forced the painful irony home, that Native Americans, the original inhabitants of this continent, had been forced out of their lands, subject to a process of colonization more brutal, if anything, than India had endured.

To be called 'Indian,' then, was to be caught in the cross-fire of the white man's naming patterns, Columbus's dream of an earthly paradise, broken, boisterous, brutal.

What could it mean to an Indian from Asia to live and breathe and move in America? To make up a self in America? Indeed, to be American, as millions of immigrants had wanted? To make a new life, a life in the ordinary world, facing daylight. What could this ceaseless present mean?

I wrote a long poem called "Ashtamudi Lake" and later pondered the last lines in the poem. Trying to move between two worlds, the vision ends in a house filled with flames.

Reading the lines again I thought, I can't bear it, this here-there business. In any case, I would choke in a house filled with flames.

So I quarreled with myself. And out of the quarrel with the self came writing.

I went walking on Broadway, at the edge of Harlem. I came upon a woman who had set out a yellow cloth on the sidewalk and on the cloth were books, ten, perhaps twelve books. Beautiful books, their covers intact.

'Why are you selling these books?' I asked the woman. 'Because my apartment is flooded,' the woman replied. 'I used to collect books, but now a pipe has burst and there is water everywhere.'

I bought a book from the woman, paid the money, and felt I was receiving a gift. It was a lovely yellow and black book with a line drawing by Pablo Picasso on the cover. Inside were poems by Aimé Césaire. The title of the book was *Corps Perdu* (Lost Body).

I held open the book and started to walk. Something was wet underfoot. A stream of water, swelling. The gutters were flooding. As I walked on, the water drained away and I saw the Hudson, risen to the edge of its banks, grey water lapping.

Memory contained, memory lowering itself to the level of the containable, so that one is not flooded over.

One of my earliest memories was of the Aswan High Dam being built in the Sudan, where I lived for many years as a child, the waters of the Nile flooding habitable ground, great faceless monuments that were rescued, the fragile brightness of the Virgin of Faras, unearthed from Nubia. That dark, slender woman, painted on plaster, the halo round her head—sheer fabrication. What memories did the Virgin of Faras hold?

I continued walking, reading Cesaire's lines as I walked:

'Tout ce qui jamais fut dechiré
en moi s'est dechiré
tout ce qui jamais fut mutilé
en moi s'est mutilé.'

(All that was ever torn/is torn in me/All that was ever mutilated/is mutilated in me.)

I thought of the scores of memories that can never be lashed back into place, the white sails on the Nile, the water lights on the Hudson, the fishermen's nets on the Pamba, gleaming in moonlight. I continued reading the poem:

'le fruit coupé de la lune toujours en allée
vers le contour à inventer de l'autre moitié.'

The vision of postcolonial invention worked its bright resonance—a slashed moon perpetually moving toward 'the invented contour of its other part.'

Walking toward the river, I understood something I had only sensed dimly: the task of making up memory. This is the dark woman's burden. As if I were wholly another self, another body, I started laughing, at first silently, then the laughter spilt out.

What she is has no ready shape. It is all still to be invented. She needs an aesthetic that can rework the discord of the senses, clarify the violations of empire.

So this is what the new world can bring. Still walking, approaching the river wall where the Hudson flows, I feel very, very old and ever so new at the same time, an ancient woman hobbling, a small child just learning to use her legs.

I think of a very old woman seated on a stool, stitching words together. Her needle is very cool. It can take the burning words. As for the small child, she must learn to walk in the dense irregularity of the city. Learn to delight in the sharp, synchronic music, rare fractals the bodily senses will forge into remembrance.

A bird cries by the river wall. The cry turns guttural, more musical. It will not cease. The bird from *Kadambari* is telling its tale. The bars of its cage become the streets of the city.

Snow starts to fall. I walk back to my room as quickly as I can. The wind is rising and the very street where I walked blurs with the falling flakes.

What I know is what I can remember. It is winter working in me, I think, as I pick up a pen and start to write poems of the cold.

San Andreas Fault

'And if I cried, who'd listen to me in those angelic orders?'

—Rilke, *Duino Elegies*

I. The Apparition

Too hard to recall each grass blade, burn of cloud
in the monsoon sky, each cata maran's black sail.
Nor very easily, could we make ourselves
whole through supplication,
before and after—the jagged rasp of time,
cooled by winds brushing the Pacific.
The brown heart, rocking, rocking,
ribs dashed to the edge of San Andreas Fault.

Suddenly I saw her, swathed in silk
seemingly weightless, nails prized into rock,
rubber boots dangling over the gorge:

'This morning light over water
drives everything out of mind, don't you agree?
I know the Ganga is like nothing else on earth
but now I fish here.
San Andreas suits me: salmon, sea perch, striped bass.'

Montara, Moss Beach, Pescadero, Half Moon Bay,
North American names quiver and flee, pink shrubs,
stalks of the madrone, speckled heather rooting in clumps
And under it all, the fault, her voice worked free:

'I watched him walking with you, holding hands in sunlight
the two of you against a wall: hands, face, eyes, all shining
he had a brown paper bag, you nothing. How come?'

Feet hot against madrone roots, veins beating indigo
to the rift where her thighs hung, musically
unbuckling gravity, I set my face to her squarely:

'Come to America so recently
what would you have me carry in my hands?
In any case why bring in a man I hardly see anymore?'

II. Flat Canvas

Once, waiting for him in the parking lot
right by the tap and muddied pool where wild dogs from the
canyon congregate—he was often late—I let the sunlight
bathe my face.
Stared into water, saw myself doubled, split,
a stick figure, two arms bloodied with a bundle racing
past parked cars of Third World immigrants.

Then I saw him sprinting by my side:
'Teeth, Teeth, Teeth'
he cried, his body bolted down
a dream by Basquiat
flat canvas, three-pronged heart, broken skull laced with spit,
skin stretched over a skeleton pierced with nails,
Gray's Anatomy in its right hand, in its left, a Bible.

In Malayalam, Hindi, Arabic, French he cried out
turning to English last, babbling as the continental coast
broke free
riveting Before and After

jump starting reflection.
The Angel of Dread, wings blown back
neck twisted over mounds of rubble,
door posts with blood of the lamb smeared on.
And faintly visible under jarring red
words like 'Progress,' 'Peace,' 'Brotherly Love,'
'One Nation under God,' all that stuff.

III. Funeral Song

I sensed his breath on my neck
he needed to suck me into eternity
press thumbs against my throat, set a paper bag
against my thighs, warm with the hot dog he got on the cheap from
the corner store by the supermarket wall.
'A real American hot dog, sauerkraut and all,' he boasted
till tears took hold.

He pressed me tight against a tree,
in full sight of an Indian family
struggling with their groceries, thrusting
harder as breath came in spurts—
a funeral song he learnt from his mother
the words from Aswan filling me:

'You have crossed a border, never to return.
Stranger in this soil, who will grant you burial?
Neck of my beloved, who will grant you burial?
Eyes, lips, nose, who will shield you from sight?'

Tighter and tighter he pressed till the fruits of the fig tree
broke loose and fit to faint I thrust my fist
through his blue cotton shirt, shook myself free.

IV. Package of Dreams

Late at night in Half Moon Bay
hair loosed to the glow of traffic lights
I slit the moist package of my dreams.

Female still, quite metamorphic
I flowed into Kali ivory-tongued, skulls nippling my breasts.
Durga lips etched with wires astride an electric tiger.
Draupadi born of flame betrayed by five brothers
Stripped of silks in the banquet hall of shame.

In the ghostly light of those women's eyes
I saw the death camps at our century's end:

A woman in Sarajevo shot to death
as she stood pleading for a pot of milk,
a scrap of bread, her red scarf swollen
with lead hung in a cherry tree.

Turks burnt alive in the new Germany,
a grandmother and two girls
cheeks puffed with smoke
as they slept in striped blankets
bought new to keep out the cold.

A man and his wife in Omdurman
locked to a starving child, the bone's right
to have and hold never to be denied,
hunger stamping the light.

In Ayodhya, in Ram's golden name
hundreds hacked to death, the domes
of Babri Masjid quivering as massacres begin—
the rivers of India rise mountainous,
white veils of the dead, dhotis, kurtas, saris,

slippery with spray, eased from their bloodiness.

V. San Andreas Fault

Shaking when I stopped I caught myself short
firmly faced her, 'What forgiveness here?'
'None,' she replied. 'Every angel knows this.'
The damage will not cease and this sweet gorge
by which you stand bears witness.

'Become like me a creature of this fault.'

She said this gently, swinging to my side
body blown to the fig tree's root.

'Stop,' I cried. 'What of this burden?
The messy shroud I stepped into?
Ghostly light? Senseless mutilations?'

Her voice worked in my inner ear
sorrow of threshed rice,
cadences of my mother tongue loosed in me:

'Consider the glory of salmon as it leaps spray
to its own death, spawn sheltered in stone
under running water.
That's how we make love—Can you understand?
Each driven thing stripping itself,
to the resinous song of egg and sap in chill water.

'Sometimes I think this is my mother's country
she conceived me here, legs splayed, smoke in her eyes
in the hot season when gold
melts from chains, beads, teeth
and even the ceremonials of the dead

dwelt on in Upper Egypt, dissolve away.

'We are new creatures here.
Hooking fish in San Andreas we return them to the fault
perch, black salmon, the lot.

'When the walls of your rented room
in Half Moon Bay fall away
consider yourself blessed.

'The snows of the Himalayas
glimpsed in your mother's songs
once came from rainclouds high above this coast
cradling the rafters of the seven heavens.'

The Shock of Arrival

Body, Memory, Desire in Asian-American Art

I went to see the exhibit *Identities in Contemporary Asian-American Art* showing at the Asia Society. Strolling through the gallery space, moving carefully around the installation pieces, stopping, gazing at paintings and mixed media pieces hung on the walls, I was struck by how much of what I saw offered a rich, aesthetic resistance to what might be thought of as the great unifying forces of America. This was art born out of dislocation, art that enshrines disjunction.

Later, indoors, at my writing desk, I look out and see fresh leaves on the trees catch the light, brownish green, bristling with sap. Somehow the words of the great philosopher Sankara come to mind: fire, something about fire. I pick up his *Vivekachudamani* and find the line:

'The world is a forest on fire!'[1]

What would it mean for the trees by the river to start burning? What would it be like to approach this coast, this river for the first time and see the trees as if aflame, smoke rising?

The shock of arrival in the new world is crucial to an understanding of contemporary Asian-American art. It crystallizes the jagged boundaries of the disjunctive worlds that the artist presses into play, and clarifies the painful gap between desire and the brute actual. It is replayed, over and over again, through the thematics of passage, arrival and dwelling, figurations that permit us to make sense, however minimally, of the rupture between desire and the actual, between intimate memories and a place where one is rendered strange, where the body is marked as Other.

What does it mean to arrive in America? From the large onggi jars of Y. David Chung's 1994 *Mega Morning Calm* that frame the entry to the Asia Society exhibit on *Identities in Contemporary Asian-American Art* to the flaming kimono in Takako Nagai's 1990 *Self-Portrait*, this question, indeed this obsession, as one might put it, refigures itself, elaborated in the specific, often haunting densities of the individual works.

Rendered Other in the new world, one is interrogated, asked who one is, made to respond. And for an artist, work that overtly occupies space forming a figuration in which one might exist, is part of the response. David Chung, in his artist's statement, picks this out: 'Because everyone calls you Korean, you try to figure out what that means by digging all the way back to early mythology and linking that to today.' Takako Nagai, who inscribed a poem over the painted image of a flaming kimono, asking where the new life will lead, writes in her brief statement: 'The identity I had, even five years ago, doesn't exist anymore.'[2]

What is one to make of this? An art forged in the crucible of unknowing, bound in by the American present. Artists who, whether they immigrated here or were born in this country, are postmodernist in their quest for identity. Yet clearly, a re-envisioning of history is part of the passage into the present, the crystallized frame that allows for aesthetic representation.

May Sun, in her installation piece *Fugitive Landing*, works her way back to Sun Yat Sen, who landed at a San Francisco pier in 1896 in his quest for Chinese communities all over the world who could organize to overthrow the imperial dynasties. On the front wall of the installation piece, we see books held by long loops, speared by knives: two volumes of John Stuart Mill's *Political Economy*; *Marx on China*; Marx's articles from the *New York Daily Tribune*; Edgar Snow's *Red Star over China*. And behind the wall, under a fine wooden trellis, waters mimicking a Chinese garden, and on the wall a projection imaging ocean waters. We hear the sound of foghorns, tapes telling of clandestine political meetings—all part of the space of transition, the liminality of arrival in the new world. Setting up visible links between knowledge and social change, May Sun's *Fugitive Landing* forces us to ponder the fluid, intersecting boundaries of past and present for an Asian-American artist, boundaries in which body, memory, and desire are crucially implicated.

Memory is painfully at work in Long Nguyen's paintings. The artist arrived in America as a teenager, after the collapse of South Vietnam. The terror of passage in an old freighter is brought out in his *Soul Boat*. The tiny craft becomes a living body with head and arms, floating in a dark and hellish water. The infernal setting was something the artist needed to convey the dread of passage, silence, darkness, secrecy. He has said of the experience that lies behind this work that it was as if 'the boat and the people on the boat became part of one body.' Again the image of one nightmarish body comes alive in his painting *Tales of Yellow Skin #1*, where a large, distended head is placed on a stick that has many other heads springing from it, the whole awash in an ochre landscape where small fires are raging.

The way memory reworks the body image is crucial to the paintings of Sisavath Panyathip, who came to America from Laos as a teenager. His memories of warfare and life in a 'reeducation camp,' his isolation in his new world result in a series of body images striking for the way in which individual features are scrubbed out and the outline of the body remains, still, anonymous. We see eyes and mouth bound with strips of paint in *First Year in the US;* a lotus and open Bible blossoming out of the body in *Baptism*—the artist's conversion to Christianity, pressed upon him by his American sponsors, existing uneasily with his Buddhism. Panyathip writes: 'I put the symbol of the lotus closer to the heart to symbolize that even though I became a Mormon, in my heart I was still a Buddhist.'

. . . .

What could be closer to me than my own body, my body image? Yet what could be more permeable to the currents of the world, the rough waves of ideology? Gender, the social construction of sexuality, flows as an intrinsic portion of this current. I see myself, to some extent, as I am seen, as bodily being. Struggling against the way I am seen, I remake myself, rework the images that encode the symbolic valencies of self. I might whisper this or shout it out aloud, but truth comes to me through the sensorium of a gendered body. The contortions of colonialism and the tension of historical memory both work for women artists through the textures of a gendered awareness. Women artists have had to contend both with how they are seen as women—given the harshness of patriarchy—and how as Asian Americans they are seen as marginal to the mainstream.

In the work of Chinese-born painter Hung Liu, the figures of women loom large. In her painting *Tang Ren Jie*, or *Tang People's Street*, the canvas is split between the image of a Chinese prostitute, her face downcast, walking down a San Francisco street at the turn of the century and an image from the Tang era, an imperial concubine. In her bold replication in *Resident Alien* we confront a massive Green Card with the artist's face and thumbprint set under the name 'COOKIE, FORTUNE.' Who is this Fortune Cookie, we might ask ourselves? Who indeed?

A woman certainly, an Asian woman struggling against both the strictures of colonialism and bonds of patriarchy.

In the photographs of Vietnam-born Hanh Thi Pham, we see a series of *tableaux vivants* in which the artist herself, in the pose of a young Vietnamese girl, engages Europeans in a mutual, incomprehensible gaze. In *Evening Stroll/Night Patrol*, a European couple gazes in at her house, while she holds up a Mickey Mouse doll for them. The doll stares back at the gazing couple. In *Reconnaissance/This House is my own House*, the artist figure spies on a mixed-race couple in their luxurious house, complete with tiger skin on the wall. In the hands of the furtive girl is a toy rifle.

Most fierce perhaps, more combative certainly, is the photograph entitled *No. 9, Expatriate Consciousness*. We face the bare-breasted figure of the artist, her hair cropped short, holding her fist up in an obscene gesture. Beneath her is an inverted image of William T. Cody, the legendary Buffalo Bill. The image has a large 'X' mark over the body of the man synonymous with the manifest destiny of the American thrust westward.

Elsewhere we witness the terror of desire. The surge of desire should hold the body to the world, render the future palpable, grant it color and scent and taste, limn it within the horizon of longing fulfilled. The repression of desire can result in mutilation, broken up body parts, severed limbs. In this art of disjunction we encounter images of the fragmented body, the mutilated body. In Phillipine-born Manuel Ocampo's painting *Heridas de la Lengua*, we face a brutalized iconic body, beheaded by its own hand. Knife held upright, blood spurting out and the pacific images of the virgin and child in the background. In Marlon Fuentes' *Face Fusion Series*, parts of two faces—one Asian, one Caucasian—dare to cohere in a surreal whole. But in his photograph entitled *Tongue*—from his *Circle of Fear* series—Fuentes gives us a severed cow's tongue, pierced with a crucifix and multiple shards of glass. The pain of mutilation, of voicelessness is brought very close.

'If I do not speak for myself, who will speak for me?' we ask, as we confront these images. And how shall I speak for myself without memory—my memory and the memories of my people, however dispersed, however distanced?

It seems to me that the powerful configurations of Asian-American art are forged in the crucible of a communal memory. And having said this, I need to add that I am not stipulating for the artist, for any artist. As a writer myself I have a horror of such injunctions. Rather, it seems to me that it is force of such memory that marks these figurations of the aesthetic in contemporary Asian-American art.

Ralph Waldo Emerson, transcendentalist and household philosopher of America, spoke of the American self as having no need of memory. He invoked life in the new world, cut free of the past, raised into the shining present. He presents us with a bed of roses. We are asked to consider them, their moment by moment existence: 'There is no time to them. There is simply the rose, it is perfect in every moment of its existence...[man] cannot be happy and strong, until he too lives with nature in the present, above time.'[3]

What might such a life mean? Life in the sublime vacancy of America—a land lying open for the white man's passage west. The native population devastated. Is this the necessary precondition for living without memory?

How does time work through us, through our bodies? Or do we swim in time as fish swim in the sea? We are creatures of passage. Our boundaries are those of mortality, the finitude of the body, fitful epiphanies of the soul. In his *Discipline and Punish*, in the context of a discussion of the political world and the power it exerts on the human being, Michel Foucault writes: 'the soul is the prison of the body.'[4] It is a line that has a powerful resonance for us as we examine the productions of artists whose lives have been marked by radical dislocation, whose works are structurally marked by an embodiment cast as Other to the dominant Eurocentric culture of America.

Indeed, Emerson's invocation to cast off memory, to live in the present above time, presupposed both gender and race, a white male self, which, however pitted by the pressures of introspection, was ultimately at the opposite ends of the social scale from an African-American slave laboring in the field, a Native American herded onto a reservation, an Asian-American working on the railroad. Would a female Emerson have been possible? One wonders. It is a question, perhaps, that we should pose to the ghost of Margaret Fuller. Or better still, to Sojourner Truth.

The living body makes a place for us, marks out the limits of dwelling. It stands as the irreducible marker of identity. This could never have been doubted by those Asians who were bound by the Naturalization Law of 1790, specifying that naturalized citizenship was reserved for whites. The law, in any case, was only codifying the brunt of general opinion. In his 1751 essay, "Observations Concerning the Increase of Mankind," Benjamin Franklin pointed out that Europeans were the 'principle body of White People.' Africans were black, Asians were 'tawney.' It was in the best interests of America to keep it white. He writes: 'Why increase the Sons of Africa by planting them in America where we have so fair an opportunity, by excluding all Blacks and Tawneys, of increasing the lovely White?'[5] This Eurocentric patterning of American culture is one that has persisted to this day. It is a patterning that the Asian-American artist is forced to confront when reckoning with the market forces that marginalize or tokenize the work, as well as in intimate dealings with human others, dealings which enforce the sometimes painful, sometimes exhilarating disjunctions enforced by such a residence on earth. 'Residence on earth'—I use the phrase borrowed from the great poet, Pablo Neruda. It evokes for me plenitude, a rich flow of nature, flora and fauna, the courtesy of custom, the grace of habitation.

But what might this mean? For so many of us, creatures of postcoloniality, inheritors of societies that have struggled for decolonization, our place in the taken for grantedness of things, whether we are speaking of nation-states or of linguistic boundaries, is fraught indeed. Yet this disjointed estate can force an exhilarating art, an art that takes as its birthright both dislocation and the radical challenge of reconceiving American space, one and the other, in a single, imaginative act.

By way of elaboration, I would like to imagine the Asian-American artist as a young child, born in this country, in New York City, or even in New Jersey, or further afield in California or Texas. I think of this growing child and her imagination as it turns against the actual limits of life. I cannot live, she thinks, in this house my parents have given me: this room, these walls, this food I must eat, these clothes they make me wear. I will make up another room, with better walls, find finer food. And the child takes up pencil and paper and starts drawing these things. The space she makes up on the paper becomes a space she enters into, a mimic reality, an empowerment. But what will become of this piece of paper? Or other pieces of paper she draws on as she grows up? Where will her art find its place?

Next I see the child pick up a piece of fruit, a stone, a bit of charcoal and start to rearrange space with these counters, so that what is set down becomes for her, on the small floor or bit of dirt where she works, a place in which to be, a virtuality.

Now speaking of her picture, of course, she cannot literally enter into it, even if she draws a door, a window, a crawl space, somewhere near the edge of the earth. But it is there for her, magically, and it changes the nature of reality. As for her installation, the stone, the piece of fruit, the charcoal she has arranged, these counters, too, revise space, interpret it afresh.

I think of Karl Marx in his "Theses on Feuerbach" arguing that though the philosophers have interpreted the world, the point is to change it. And confronting these lines that I read ever so many years ago, as a young woman in India, I ask myself, is it not possible that by interpreting the world, we might also change it? Why should art, which makes images of the world and of ourselves in the world, not be complicit, and powerfully so, in the charge of changing things as they are? Stripping apart the skin of what is rendered up as natural and revealing its constructed nature, adding to the store of what is given and so changing the whole count?

Art as dwelling, as making a habitable space. This is an ancient practice, stretching from the paintings of deer and buffalo on the dark walls of prehistoric caves, through the fecund forms of tree and leaf and fruit one finds in the chalk and rice drawings on the thresholds of Indian homes, the art of kolum or rangoli, through the spiritual intricacies of Navajo sand paintings. How is dwelling reconceived in Asian-American art? We have spoken, albeit briefly, about passage, about the shock of arrival. But what of dwelling? There are several artists who configure the taut tranquillity of dwelling spaces.

Zarina, an artist born in India, now living in New York City and California, puts it quite simply and beautifully: 'You draw this space around yourself,' she says, 'and it becomes your house.' The childlike simplicity of this statement is belied in the sophistication of her *House on Wheels*, twenty-five metal images of freestanding houses mounted on wheels—a symbol both of passage and stillness. A freestanding sculptural form of the house, entitled "I went on a journey," is set by the mounted images. One notices the distressed quality of the bronze, the ridges against which the light shines. The abstract form of the house, a dwelling in motion, resonates, making for a calm and tranquil repetition. The post-Enlightenment dichotomy between inside and outside, private and public is exploded. Here, inside and outside become one. The disruptions of migrancy work their way into a quiescent beauty.

A different figuration of dwelling space emerges in the work of Korean-born Jin Soo Kim. In her installations, we encounter the detritus of cities, the garbage of an industrial world reclaimed, set within the aesthetic space—an old kitchen cabinet papered on the inside with formica, set in a metal cage. In her mixed media installation *years, instants,* we see inside a metal cage a stuffed armchair, the cloth peeling off its surface. Tall steel cages hold metal pestles in them. These mute, caged objects rework the notion of a dwelling space as we reflect on the long shadows cast by inanimate objects, the terrible waste of postindustrial societies. Yet this work is also an act of celebration, of healing the dislocation suffered by the artist. 'By picking up the skin of this culture,' Jin Soo Kim writes, 'I feel I'm becoming part of this reality.'

There is a haunting elegaic quality to the installation piece *Dwelling* by the Korean-born artist Yong Soon Min. A hanbok, a fine white Korean dress, is suspended over a scaffolding of wire. It is lit from within by light bulbs and floats gently over a stack of eleven books, all bound in white. The twelfth book, closest to the hanbok, is burnt. Ash spills onto the floor and, all the while, the white transparency above is floating, floating. 'This work,' writes Yong Soon, 'embodies my active preoccupation with the notion of finding a place for myself.'

Finding a place for oneself is also critical to the work of Pacita Abad, the Phillipine-born artist. In her acrylic, oil and collage piece on canvas, *How Mali Lost Her Accent*, the poignant figure of Mali stares out at us. Round her neck is a Benetton purse; behind and around her, the facades of great institutions of higher learning: Harvard, Yale, UCLA, and Columbia. Like a series of tombstones in front of her stands a set of computers with instructions to 'Perfect her Words, Manage her Money.' What does it mean to find one's place in America? What does finding a place mean for an Asian-American artist who bears within him or herself the marks of radical migrancy? I think of the fragile boats made of wood and other substances by the Thailand-born Toi Ungkavatanapong; the fierce metal bed jutting off the wall at an impossible angle, forged by the China-born artist Baochi Zhang; the suitcase filled with kimchee jars in the installation by Korean-born Sung Ho Choi; the bitter foam core and acrylic pop art of Ken Chu, born in China, living in America. The title of one of them, *Hey Chinktown! You killed my father*, refuses to leave me. What kind of place can such artists find in America?

The answer is not simple. Place, itself, must be radically reworked, the idea of America re-envisaged. And it is precisely this project of radical re-envisioning that these works of art and many others like them are implicitly engaged in. I say implicitly, for we are in the realm of the aesthetic rather than the realm of rhetoric. Through our encounters with these works, through the shock of arrival that they crystallize, a phenomenology of Asian-American art might be traced.

I need to curve back and briefly lay out what I mean by the shock of arrival, which we are now proposing as part of the phenomenology of the Asian-American work of art. Frequently, the images of passage give way to the complexity of arrival. Arrival then renders itself up as dwelling, the preservation of being in place, preservation that cannot be cleft from the multitude of memories that jostle the living body. And where the body exists, there one finds desire, the glue that holds us to the future, the passion, the fiery junction in a world of rupture.

Aesthetic meaning in such a phenomenology cannot be cleft apart from the tension of place. These works, through their various and deliberately fragmented forms, resist the universalizing notion of America as a vast, unified culture, seamless, equitable. Through the sharp memories that jostle canvas, foam core and bronze, paper, steel, and scrap metals, cloth and books, these multimedia works and many others like them challenge and rework pre-existing frames of identity. By occupying space, they force us to revision the shared world.

Standing as we do in the shadow of the Quincentennial, such awareness is not irrelevant to our psychic survival, to our cultural vitality. Five hundred years after Christopher Columbus's 'discovery' of America, one thinks back to the man's obsession with finding India, his certitude that he had gotten there, even when mad and raving, he was carted back to Europe. One thinks of the way in which the Native Americans became prey to a violence more brutal than any they could have conceived of, the arrival of the Spanish ships presaging an end to the rights to land, to freedom, to community.

There is another piece of this story I would like to tell. And it touches the part of Asia I come from. In 1498, six years after Columbus touched North America, Vasco da Gama landed in Calicut, on the Kerala coast, a city where, a century ago, my mother's mother was born. As a child growing up in India, I learnt of how the Portuguese, approaching the Indian coast, set fire to a ship, all souls aboard burnt alive, as a signal of European power. Later, I learnt of how, in the 16th century, the Portuguese conducted an Inquisition on the Syrian Christians who lived on the Kerala coast. The Europeans burnt the palymra leaf of the sacred scriptures, defaced the copper tablets, tortured believers, since they thought them heretics. Coming to America, I put Columbus and Vasco da Gama together in my imagination, the quest for the mythic Asia and the violence it bred. As Asian-American artists, we are heirs to this legacy, too.

Indeed, the theme of violence is not irrelevant to these postcolonial musings. Frantz Fanon, the visionary of decolonization, was forced to make violence in multiple forms the centerpiece of his anguished work, *The Wretched of the Earth*. Writing during the Algerian war of independence, he argued that colonialism was 'violence in its natural state.'[6] In his passionate way, he spoke out about the cleansing force of a counterviolence, one that the forces of decolonization must necessarily use. Yet at the end of his book, in the chapter on "Colonial Wars and Mental Disorders," Fanon himself reveals the radical instability of violence, the terrible cycle of dread in which both victim and perpetrator are bound. Indeed, for Fanon, in opposition to a great figure such as Mohandas Gandhi—who developed the notion of *satyagraha* (the way of truth) as the active embodiment of nonviolent resistance to British rule—colonial violence and its terrible consequences cannot be cleft apart.

The question remains, how is the world to be changed? Art, it seems to me, even when it plunges headfirst into the destructive element, is part of our collective nonviolent resistance. Indeed, some might argue that swimming in the destructive element is part of the necessary passage of the artist. At the tail end of the century, it is part and parcel of our project of creating a shared dwelling place. In its response to this challenge, contemporary Asian-American art becomes part of our essential knowledge.

If the world outside, the trees bristling in the spring wind, the grey ribbon of the West Side Highway, all seem to be on fire, one must say so, conceive it as so, paint it as such, so that our shared culture strips apart its skin, revises its ferment to include us.

I would like to end with a poem, which comes out of my own life. It is set in Long Island City, in Isamu Noguchi's museum, a meditation on some of these themes of disjunction that we have touched on. I composed it during the Gulf War, which was also an Asian war, involving the massive dislocation and relocation of workers from South and Southeast Asia, out of Iraq and Kuwait. Indeed, it is not irrelevant that, from the perspective of India, both Iraq and Kuwait are considered part of West Asia.

The poem moves from Noguchi's museum and garden to Sabermati Ashram in Ahmedabad, India. A meditation on art that traces lines across the world, it is an elegy to the Gujarati poet, Uma Shankar Joshi, who was a friend to me.

Paper Filled with Light

In memory of Uma Shankar Joshi (1911-1989)

I.

Under a plum tree, a stone that weeps water
under a roof of wood, paper filled with light
Noguchi understood this emptiness, this discipline
his father's blackening heart he turned to sheer stone

A circlet for our hands titled Sun at Midnight
or Spirit's Flight, cool torsion cut to Carrara marble

I whisper these things to you as I stand in Isamu's garden
in cool September, under a plum tree, wanting to add
in my usual way—here, in another country—as if
the germ of death were on my tongue already

But there's no distance between us now; you who lived
by the word are wholly immortal, your lines burnt into history.

II.

Under a plum tree, a stone that weeps water
in Setu, under a roof of wood, paper filled with light

You clarified this discipline, seizing emptiness

the precise weights of the palpable
fired by the fury of sight, speech arced to the extremities
of the known, fronting the axe of displacement:

The massacres of '47, the killing fields of Partition,
Gandhi, his eyes burnt into prayers—He fasted,
we all did in those days, fasting for peace—
In '84 in Trilokpuri a girl child raped, stabbed in the riots,

Her mother bent over a cooking pot trembling,
mouth stuffed with stones. Poetry as witness:
silk torn so the blackness of the frame can remember
the limbs, the bloodied stuff that makes us a nation.

III.

Above the plum tree, this northern sky is streaked with pink
almost as if we were in Gandhi's ashram
by rocks with mouths ruder than plum stones
by water so empty it takes color from the sky

In the dry season before the river splintered
before you pitched yourself into a dream so steep
your daughters could not clamber down the edge
to hook father's syllables from whorled water, blackest ink.

IV.

Uma Shankar, I ask you now, what is the sun at midnight?
The spirit's flight? The gold roof of heaven?

What is death doing in the throats of those
from your Bamna, my Tiruvella crouched in Jordan's deserts?

What is death scribbling on their cheeks
as they stumble to a water truck long run dry?

I am here in Isamu's garden, by an old warehouse,
by a children's park, by the East River—rusty gasoline tanks, the
packed cars of new immigrants, the barbed wires
of Meerut, Bensonhurst, Baghdad, strung in my brain.

How could I sing of a plum tree, a stone that weeps water?
How could I dream of paper filled with light?

Fracturing the
Iconic Feminine

In their struggle to reach the sources of creative power, Indian women writers had to confront the iconic presentation of the feminine, fracture and reform it. This confrontation took on added complexity when the struggle was part of the effort to decolonize. But how is feminine consciousness to be torn free? How is colonialism, so intimately absorbed by the writer, to be taken apart? I need to ask these questions as part of my own struggle with history, with memory, with what it means to be born into a female body. In my quest for my own voice, I had to turn back to women who have written as part of an earlier generation in India.

The predicament of women writers confronting the strictures of an unjust power, whether close to home, indeed making up part and parcel of the inner shelters of domesticity—I am thinking now of the hierarchical ordering of a patriarchal family and the demands of a culturally constructed masculinity—or facing the corrosive demands of a colonial power, makes visible for us a double bondage through which female creativity must work its way. A double peril that incites the woman's imagination to realms of almost inconceivable freedom.

Often there are two voices or two strains of thought that will not work harmoniously into a single, shimmering web. The disjunction between the iconic feminine, the culturally sanctioned image of woman, and that other more ferocious, more disruptive power without which one could not write, threatens to tear apart the constructed fabric of the work, force it askew vis-à-vis the realm of actuality.

What do I mean by this? I mean that for the woman writer born into the colonial or even the postcolonial era, the effort to cut through that subtle, often infinitely pernicious fabric is part and parcel of the reaching out for form—for a form that does not buy into the previously sanctioned ideologies of poetry or prose. She is forced, then, to forge what I might call, for want of a better phrase, *a back against the wall aesthetic*. The formal structures she uses may well seem crude, since they are forged with what lies close to hand, and the living body, in all its passionate instrumentality, becomes the pivot of expressive truth.

The woman writer, then, if she has grown to full maturity, finds herself creating a work that does not necessarily hold together in the requirements of an established aesthetic. Then, too, she is conscious of working with materials that have no previously sanctioned place, either in her own traditional society or in the formalities of a borrowed aesthetic. Indeed, when she is from a traditional, hierarchical society, she must come to terms with varieties of displacement, some more violent than others, as well as the poise of a ritualized order.

And the questions of a lasting freedom, of a sublime transcendence that so often haunts the imagination, do not vanish. On the contrary, they take on an added edge, since they seem so close, indeed inseparable from the figures of a previously sanctioned femininity, a borrowed, archaic language in which one has so often figured forth one's intimate self. Tragically, the cost for the easing of such constraints can sometimes be the loss of the body's hold on the world, seat of sensuous perception.

So what of those two voices I mentioned earlier? For the woman writer confronting both the masculine hierarchies of her world and the injustices of colonialism, those voices, rather than being split along the lines of a dual imposition, sexism and colonialism, run multiple, turbulent notes together, casting a self-enclosed feminine, sanctified by ritual and tradition against turbulent desires, tearing apart the skin of things as they are.

And it is the skin of things as they are and the fierce, outcaste power of the female imagination that one needs to talk about. The social constructions of a hierarchical society in which woman is ritually displaced and the humiliations of a colonial order force consciousness forward: toward a reality that has no readily conceivable form. For when what is given as natural needs to be torn apart, language becomes as vulnerable as skin, and the body, quivering in its newness, must lay itself open to fresh forms of otherness.

Whether in the case of Sarojini Naidu, born in 1879 and writing in English, the colonial language, or Lalithambika Antherjanam and Nalapat Balamaniamma, born in the first decade of the 20th century and working in Malayalam, their mother tongue, female identity was forced to survive what was at times an almost unbearable tension between a culturally sanctioned femininity and the claims of female imaginative power. When the former splintered beyond recognition, the woman writer found herself fearfully, perilously, working toward a new world. In Naidu's case, her imaginative quest landed her right at the heart of political turmoil, a world her earlier poems seemed to have no connection with.

In Search of
Sarojini Naidu

In 1977 I started work at the University of Hyderabad, in the gracious white building, 'The Golden Threshold' where the poet Sarojini Naidu had lived. I was determined to find out as much as I could about her life and had started talking with a filmmaker friend about a script of her life. My first book of poetry, a cycle of poems, had come out the previous year and I was struck by the words of a reviewer: 'lyrical, in the Sarojini Naidu vein.' I knew that the reputation of the famous woman of Indian politics, 'the Nightingale of India,' had fallen on hard times. In the '70s, in the small world of Indian poetry written in English, her poetry was held to be of little account, even though her political contribution could hardly be denied.

Sarojini Naidu grew up in the interface of two cultures: that of Hyderabad, where she was born, and the colonial culture of British India. Born of Bengali parents in the city of Hyderabad, she spoke not Bengali but Urdu, the Islamic language of culture in her city. Living at the edge of Bengali and espousing Urdu, Naidu added English to her store, the language of British India. It provided the medium for both her poetry and her political speeches.

But there are hard questions to ask of her poetry and politics. Was there an impossible cleft between the intense, if imprisoning passions of her poetry and the political life she espoused? The self she forged through political action, did it draw in any way on the anguished images she picked up from turn of the century English poetry? And what of the dichotomy between poet

and politician, scarcely to be explained, pointing toward complicated, covert procedures of creativity? And then her use of English. How had she been able to put the language of colonialism to
such intimate use? What had it cost her? Why had she stopped
writing poems?

English has, of course, been an immensely controversial issue for Indian writers. Sarojini Naidu first came to the public eye
as a poet in English, the colonial language her father forced her to
learn. Yet it was English that Naidu used in both her poetry and
political speeches. In her public oratory, she was able to cut herself loose of the passive, weak images of femininity she had
drawn from turn of the century British poetry and move forwards into a powerful attack on colonialism.

Naidu met Mohandas Gandhi in London in 1914 and recalls
in her writing how she saw 'a little man with a shaven head,
seated on the floor on a black prison blanket and eating a messy
meal of squashed tomatoes and olive oil out of a wooden prison
bowl. Around him were ranged some battered tins of parched
ground nuts and tasteless biscuits of dried plantain. I burst in-
stinctively into happy laughter...'[1] Their friendship strengthened
her nationalist instincts and, in 1930, five years after she was
elected president of the Indian National Congress, Naidu found
herself leading Gandhi's Salt March.

At the crack of dawn, on April 6, 1930, Gandhi and his com-
pany went down to the sea to bathe. Then he gathered up in his
palms a few grains of the salt that had dried on the beach, symbolic defiance of the British salt law that held a monopoly on the
production of salt in India. Thousands followed him, women too,
bearing earthenware and metal pots in which the salt water was
borne away. The salt, once dried, was auctioned off, quite pub-
licly, nature itself harnessed in the struggle for national freedom.

On May 5, Gandhi was arrested and the leadership of the
nonviolent movement fell to Sarojini Naidu. With 25,000 volunteers, she approached Darshana, determined to enter the salt
works. It was hot and dry, and the volunteers suffered from a terrible thirst. The police were ranged to meet them and beat them

with lathis, often violently, over the head. Naidu never flinched. She addressed the volunteers, prayed with them, and at times to keep her strength going, sat in a small deck chair writing or spinning khadi.[2] As bit by bit the volunteers who courted arrest fell to the police blows, Naidu sat calm, keeping watch. By mid-month, she herself was arrested and carted off to jail.

She suffered frequent imprisonment, the most lengthy and painful being in 1942 after the Quit Indian Resolution when she, together with Gandhi and his wife, Kasturba, was incarcerated in the Aga Khan Palace. Sickness and inaction haunted them all. In February of the following year, while still imprisoned, Kasturba, who had been suffering from a slow, prolonged fever, died. After her death, Gandhi was released. Naidu herself, suffering from malarial fever, was set free on March 21, 1943, aged sixty-four.

Despite her great political prominence, it was as a poet that Sarojini Naidu first entered the public realm. Yet her images of private, pained women suffering emotional deprivation, even psychic imprisonment, stand in direct contrast to the public life she fearlessly espoused. In the cause of national freedom, starting as early as 1903, she traveled countless miles, campaigning in her strong orator's voice all over India.

Was she able to cauterize her private pain through her poems and then move outwards into the public sphere? Or did the poems, with their sometimes cloying diction, their female figures trapped in an unredeemed sexuality, force her to leave them behind, the writer herself consumed more and more by the political struggle, so that by 1917 she effectively stopped writing?

Her first book of poems, *The Golden Threshold,* was published in London in 1905. Its frontispiece was a pen-and-ink drawing by W. B. Yeats: 'June 1896' appears under the clearly legible signature. The face of the young woman, her posture upright though not stiff, is grave, composed. Her eyes are dark, etched firmly under the straight brows. Her hair is tied back. The hands clasped above the chest form a graceful line to the chin. The shoulders are erect. In this line drawing, both the gravity and the innocence of the adolescent are visible. Sarojini was only fifteen when she was sent off to England on a scholarship from the Nizam of Hyderabad. She had indiscreetly fallen in love with a Dr. Naidu, far older than her, and of the wrong caste. She had to be got out of the country. The portrait was made at the end of her sojourn abroad.

The Golden Threshold was published with an introduction by Arthur Symons, an established man of letters by the time the volume appeared. He tells us that the volume is being published at his 'persuasion.' His awe at the 'mystic' Orient and concern with the exotic emerge in his lengthy description of her eyes, which he says concentrate all her beauty, in his glowing descriptions, too, of her 'clinging dresses of Eastern silk' and her 'long, black hair.' Interwoven with Symons' praise for the 'agony of sensation' in this young woman are extracts from her letters from Hyderabad in which she reveals just how she came to use the English language with all the fluency, even euphony, that Symons and others so admired. Sarojini tells of how she was 'stubborn and refused to speak' English. Her father, a famous chemist whose obsession was alchemy, locked his daughter up, all alone in a room, for a whole day. She was a child of nine at the time and the letter, written years later, conveys the shock of this first punishment: 'I came out of it a full-blown linguist. I have never spoken any other language to him or my mother, who always speaks to me in Hindustani.'[3]

What was working in her mind, one wonders—the cruelty of the locked room, the enforced learning, through which she worked her most intimate feelings, a strange duty honed to the bone, in a painful monolingualism? She acquired English, the language of colonization, via the closed room, forerunner of the prisons she was forced to inhabit as an activist in the National movement. And she chose deliberately to speak to both parents in that language, both father and mother, severed from her through the language of both punishment and accomplishment.

Indeed her early poetry, and all her poetry was composed in English, establishes a theme never overcome in her career as a writer—feminine selves, that endure mutilation, are psychically imprisoned. One thinks of the feminine figures in a poem like "Pardah Nashin": their days behind the veil are described as 'a revolving dream'; their clothing, idealized, unreal becomes 'morning mist/Shot opal, gold and amethyst.'[4] The stasis Naidu evokes is not so far from that of her English contemporaries, an Ernest Dowson or Symons enthralled by the deathly passivity in which a woman must be fixed. In his poem "Morbidezza," for instance, Symons in full flourish as a Decadent celebrates a 'White girl,' her 'flesh as lilies' under a 'frozen moon.' In 'Maquillage' he describes in detail the artifice of a woman, her 'rouge on fragile cheeks/Pearl-powder, and about the eyes/The dark and lustrous Eastern dyes.'[5] Both poems appeared in *Silhouettes*, a volume whose second edition appeared in 1896, when Sarojini was still in England.

The young Sarojini learnt her lesson all too well, embracing for herself the world-weary sensations, the stasis, the unmistakable agony of women who have nowhere to go. The irony is that she should learn from Symons or Dowson, carrying their diction back to India, using in her poetry images of exhausted women, hermetically sealed, a double colonization that the interchange of cultures drew her to.

In "Suttee," she goes a step further. The voice is that of a woman mourning the death of her beloved husband and it is clear that as a mere blossom she cannot survive without his strength, the 'tree of my life.' In the culminating stanza, there is a terrible self-destruction the woman takes to herself, her own subjectivity mere 'flesh' from which the 'soul'—the male beloved's life—has been cleft.

The language of dualism—flesh vs. soul, substance vs. sense—rises up to buttress the unequal divisions of gender. Lacking soul, the woman, mere flesh, must die. This poem is clearly in the tradition of William Wordsworth's "Ruined Cottage," where Margaret, abandoned by her husband, Robert, must die and of Alfred Lord Tennyson's "Lady of Shallot," the death of the woman in each case essential to the perfection of the lyric poem.

The Romanticism imposed by a British colonial education has borne strange fruit.

When *The Golden Threshold* appeared in 1905, Naidu was a young woman of twenty-six, married, with four young children. But far from being content to remain within the walls of the home she shared with her husband, she moved outwards, into the political realm. In December 1904, at the eighteenth session of the Indian National Congress—a large portion of which was devoted to issues of women's rights, like education, purdah, child marriage, and polygamy—Naidu met some of the great reformers of her day, including the powerful Ramabai Ranade, who presided over the women's sessions. For her part, Naidu recited the patriotic "Ode to India," which was much appreciated at this first public reading.[6] At the center of the poem lies the image of India as a 'slumbering Mother' who must be awoken by her daughter's cry. While in a poem like "Suttee" the bond to the male renders the woman helpless, here the longing to awaken the mother quickens a desire for empowerment, political myth intersecting with subjective need. The ancient earth is still able to 'Beget new glories' and the idealized past is drawn into the quest for an equally idealized future: 'Mother, O Mother, wherefore dost thou sleep?/Arise and answer for thy children's sake!...Waken O slumbering Mother and be crowned,/Who once wert empress of the sovereign past.'

It is as if the daughter, by awakening the mother, were able to free herself from imprisoning passion. The image of India as mother struck a deep vein in the culture. *Punya bhumi* (blessed earth) and *Bharat mata* (mother India) were linked together for poet and audience. The mother was sacred, potent, terrible to her foes when awoken. In a later poem, Naidu celebrates 'Kali the mother,' fierce, passionate goddess of both life and destruction: 'O terrible and tender and divine!/O mystic mother of all sacrifice,' opens the poem that ends with the invocation, 'Kali! Maheshwari!'

The association with British colonialism provides a telling twist to the pervasive femaleness of the Indian earth. Citations from Keshub Chunder Sen, one of the major figures of the Bengal Renaissance, reveal how the trope acquires symbolic significance for anticolonial activity. Sen, who had visited England in 1870, was immensely taken with English culture and longed to unite Britain and India, Christianity and Hinduism. In his extended figure, India becomes the bride and England the groom: 'Let India, beloved India be dressed in all her jewelry...The bridegroom is coming.' But by 1883, the image turns into that of sexual violation. In Sen's "Asia's Message to Europe," the mother earth is a woman raped, a prisoner, violated and bleeding: 'The rivers that run eastward and the rivers that run westward are crimson with Asiatic gore...'[7]

If Sen's tragic realization provides a momentary insight into the symbolic femaleness of India, Naidu drew on that symbolism to empower her growing sense of feminist commitment. In 1906, when she spoke to the Indian Social Conference in Calcutta, there was a causal connection between the deprivation of rights that Indian women suffered and the success of the British colonizers. Her language is fierce and direct. The liberation of India is held to be inseparable from the liberation of its women. The soul, when evoked, is firmly placed in female flesh and linked to the radical powers of maternity:

'Does one man dare to deprive another of his birthright to God's pure air which nourishes his body? How then shall a man dare to deprive a human soul of its immemorial inheritance of liberty and life? And yet my friends, man has so dared in the case of Indian women. That is why you men of India are today what you are: because your fathers in depriving your mothers of that immemorial birthright have robbed you, their sons, of your just inheritance. Therefore I charge you, restore to your women their ancient rights...'[8]

As in "Ode to India," the idealized Vedic past, a dangerous device as we have seen in current developments in Indian political life (it can be used in the cause of religious extremism), stands in for the mythic golden age. Naidu was famed as an orator throughout India and, in many of her speeches, the deprivation suffered by the women around her, and by her own self in its most private portions, comes to figure as the ground of change. Restoration of women's rights becomes a necessary condition for national freedom.

Often in the poems, however, a woman's pain is conveyed as a portion of things as they are, without reference to possible change; the telling seems to suffice. Why is this so? Why was Naidu unable to break free of the choke hold of a lyricism that, while evoking female pain, could not free into the possibility of change? Was it because the ideology she drew on through the mythologized past turned the suffering female body into a transcendent object of desire, rendering it static, guiltless? In the poem "Nasturtiums," for instance, the speaker evokes the bitter fragrance of the bloom then moves on to a recitation of the names of women from Hindu mythology. Each of the women—Savitri, Sita, Draupadi, Damayanti, Shakuntala— has suffered pain or betrayal at the hands of a man. The poet's footnote points them out as 'immortal women of Sanskrit legend and song' who still 'inspire' the lives of Indian women. The tale of Sita, in particular, haunted Naidu, especially the portion of her life set forth in the disputed Uttarama Kanda of the Ramayana. There, King Rama, still dubious about her virtue after the years of exile he has forced on her, requires Sita to undergo a test by fire. Sita, white haired now and the mother of grown twins, their faces the spitting image of Rama's own, is utterly humiliated. She cries out to the mother earth and the earth, quite literally her mother, splits open to save her. Sita is swallowed back into the earth from which she emerged (King Janaka, her father, had discovered her as an infant while a field was being ploughed).

Yet Naidu was to put this myth, with its base in the maternity of the earth, to startling political use. In her work with Gandhi and C. F. Andrews to prevent the abuse of indentured women laborers who were taken from India to South Africa and Fiji, Naidu makes covert use of the fate of Sita. The godly figure of Rama, in his role as cruel husband, is elided and the British rulers take his place: 'I...raise my voice,' cries Naidu in a speech of 1917, 'not for the men, but for women, for those women whose proudest memory it is that Sita would not stand the challenge to her honor, but called upon the mother earth to avenge her and the earth opened up to avenge her.' [9]

Nineteen-seventeen saw the publication of Naidu's last volume of poetry, *The Broken Wing*. She was thirty-eight. After it, though she might have scribbled a few lines from time to time, she never seriously wrote poetry. Her life was consumed by the rigors of public campaigning, her years punctuated by imprisonment. She was known throughout India as a major political figure. This last volume culminates in a long poem called "The Temple," a poem of undeniable eroticism that the epigram from Rabindranath Tagore ('My passion shall burn as the flame of Salvation') cannot quite mask. One gathers that the poem caused quite a stir when the volume first appeared. There were rumors of illicit love or a sexual passion that the poet could not wholly fulfill in her life. In a poem called "The Secret," a portion of "The Temple," the repression of desire is so terrible that the speaker is already dead. Passion unrequited has killed her. People come forward, bearing tribute, powerless to tell of the death within her. In a perfect masking of her post-humous condition, she is visible to them, as if completely alive. But her heart was flung 'to serve wild dogs for meat' and all that is left is 'the ravening fire/Of my own heart's desire.' Terror at the impasse she has reached turns her paradoxically to celebration—if all else is lost, she must affirm the trespassing passion. In a poem called "The Sanctuary," she writes of her soul 'Flung like a pebble thro' burning space'— the punishment for her 'passionate sin.' Gender works its odd corrosions, for even as the woman falls, the male beloved is held blameless, secure in 'God's mystic garden.' His lack of sexual response, his chilling neutrality, come to stand as virtue, while she, fierce and tender, must be thrust out. One line stands out in relief: 'My outlawed spirit shall crave no pardon.'

Standing outside the laws of the world, she gathers strength through defiance, the very strength the political woman needs to work against colonial will. It is possible, then, to think of her romantic torment as creating a shock of resistance the political self can drawn on.

Yet "The Temple" does not end there. The very last portion of the poem gives us 'Devotion,' where the previous image of female flesh thrown to the dogs returns with a vengeance. And the outlawed self works into an all too earthly desecration: 'Take my flesh to feed your dogs if you choose...Am I not yours, O love to cherish or to kill?'

The poetic self is in the grip of a sexuality so atavistic that desire equals destruction. Effectively, there were no more poems. Naidu's political self, however, flourished. In 1925 she reached the height of her fame when she became the first Indian woman to be elected president of the National Congress. At her inauguration, she was led to the podium in a great procession that included Gandhi and the two Nehrus, father and son, Motilal and Jawaharlal. She acknowledged the honor done to her as a 'generous tribute to Indian womanhood.' Indeed, as a woman, she wanted nothing more than to propose a 'most modest domestic programme.' It was one she was willing to die for: 'to restore to India her true position as the supreme mistress in her own home. ...It will be my lovely though difficult task, through the coming year, to set my mother's house in order...'[10]

But this image of the maternal home, the locus of earliest nurturing and care, should not be interpreted as quiescent, for Naidu goes on in her speech to argue for resolute, even warlike measures to combat the British, measures that were in conflict with Gandhi's posture of total ahimsa. She wanted compulsory military training for all children, remobilization of the villages, and the organization of urban workers so that both women and men could arm themselves. This arming of the nation against colonialism seemed to her a 'natural and indispensable auxiliary of political emancipation.' It seemed to her that there was no other way of overthrowing the enemy that lay both within and without: those 'deadly forces of repression that challenge our human rights of liberty.'[11] Now the passage of her resistance seems clear. The confrontation with the sometimes bruising bonds of her own culture empowered her, permitting her to attack the public boundaries laid down by a colonial power. And it is possible to see that her private, often agonizing conflicts, as recorded in poetry, were crucial to the integrity of her living voice.

Gandhi and Women: Cutting Hair

When one thinks of the participation of women in the Indian Nationalist movement, Gandhi's shadow is everywhere. His genius was that he was able to fuse his vision of nonviolence with a notion of just action. For the women and men of India, it was just and proper and in keeping with dharma, just moral action, to struggle to overthrow the British. And in his own way, Gandhi was a great believer in women. His feminism, though, was of a curious sort. It was absolutely homespun and quite revolutionary. Even while believing in the maintenance of woman's place in the domestic sphere, he was able to mobilize women throughout the country in a way that had never been possible before and still has not been quite possible since.[12] But even as women were freed for political action, the female body had to bear a pitiful burden of repressed desire and the pain of withdrawn sexuality.

His call to liberate women from their realm of domesticity and draw them into the public world of action had a strong response from women all over India, who heeded the call for satyagraha. Clearly, for Gandhi, to free women into action could work toward a justification of his own larger effort. The aggressive colonial powers could be overturned by a mobilization of people who drew upon the feminine strategy of nonviolence. Still, as Madhu Kishwar has argued, Gandhi preferred to stress the moral superiority of female suffering rather than a woman's ability to enter into the public world.[13] Instead of playing on the aggressive courage of a warrior queen like the Rani of Jhansi, Gandhi chose to stress the love and internalized suffering of a Sita. Yet, with his quick ability to respond to the currents of thought around him, he argued that remaking a Sita or Savritri should never imply feminine subservience. Sita's great power was moral; even Ravana had not dared to touch her. And this moral or spiritual force could never be confused with mere passivity or helplessness.

Maternal care could provide the key to just action. Indeed, Gandhi sometimes thought of himself as a mother. This identification was possible because the land itself, drawing on ancient mythic roots, was figured forth as maternal. The image of Mother India, introduced by Bankimchandra Chatterjee into nationalist discourse, was part of the myth-making essential to decolonization. Mother India was tender, nurturing, but also explosive and virile in a manner that has no visible analogue in the Western humanist tradition. But if the concepts of maternity and maternal care were not alien to the spirit of satyagraha—indeed Gandhi took to himself concrete acts of domesticity and nurture—it was a curious sort of mothering, one which even as it inspired countless women was based on a corrosive view of female sexuality.

Quite centrally, the human body was involved in Gandhi's experiments with truth. The overt, symbolic austerities of clothing and diet, purification of passion through abstinence, the turning of the body into an instrument of just moral action, were integral to the vision of a man who had the moral courage to turn his own preoccupations with social justice to the nationalist effort at decolonization. In his attempt, then, to break the 'mind-forged manacles,' Gandhi was forced to work through the intricacies of his own psyche. But like the Romantic poet William Blake, from whom I borrow the phrase that so aptly describes the internalization of oppression, Gandhi bore within himself vestiges of an old order, an oppressive mode of thinking that infiltrated his vision of sexual desire.

On Tolstoy Farm in South Africa, where he conducted his first real experiment in communal living, Gandhi decided to let the young boys and girls bathe together: 'I had fully explained the duty of self-restraint to the children, who were all familiar with my Satyagraha doctrine. I knew, and so did the children, that I loved them with a mother's love.'[14]

He continues in explanation of the protective maternal powers he took on himself: 'My eye always followed the girls as a mother's eye would follow a daughter.' One day, however, he hears that two girls are being teased by young men. Presumably, the teasing was sexual in nature. Gandhi as narrator does not go into details. None seem necessary to him. His direct allusion to the Ramayana and the well-worn image of Sita's inviolable purity are used to explain his actions. He wishes to mark the female body—and here the argumentation defies all except the logic of sexual punishment—in order that the boys might learn:

'I wished the two girls to have some sign on their person as a warning to every young man that no evil eye might be cast upon them, and as a lesson to every girl that no one dare assail their purity. The passionate Ravana could not so much as touch Sita with evil intent while Rama was thousands of miles away. What mark should the girls bear so as to give them a sense of security and at the same time to sterilize the sinner's eye? This question kept me awake for the night.'

The implicit conflation of Rama with Gandhi himself, the latter so close at hand, so 'maternal,' his gaze blurring into that of the young man, permits him to justify his next step: scapegoating the female body. Though the older women protest, Gandhi finally brings them round to his point of view and they allow him to cut off the 'fine long hair' of the two young girls. The 'double shame' he spoke of so lucidly in his autobiography—his father dying while Mohandas was making love to his young wife, Kasturba, who was heavily pregnant at the time; the child born weak, barely surviving for three or four days—has borne strange fruit in this episode of violence against the female body, object of sexual desire.[15]

One is forced to conclude that, in this particular instance, Gandhi's use of the maternal persona hardly serves the ends of moral justice, working rather to grant him a dubious authority, patriarchal in nature and coercive in fact. In actual fact, there was nothing simple or straightforward about the use of the maternal image for the purposes of decolonization. The complexities of human sexuality had to be faced and a price paid for the meanings constructed by the culture. And women writers, often mothers in fact and not merely image, had to struggle through the cultural validations of their estate, into an imaginative intimacy with their own bodily selves. It was a world in which murdering the mother might even seem essential to psychic growth.

In her rage at her brother who cannot permit himself to mourn a wife who abandoned him in order to follow Gandhi, Thankam, the narrator of Lalithambika Antherjanam's *Agnisakshi*, bursts out: 'Dharma! Why do you always talk about dharma when you are cornered? This dharma which does not adjust itself to changing times, let it go its way. If you are asked to kill your own mother, will you obey that also?'

It was a question the poet Nalapat Balamaniamma would try to answer.

Nalapat Balamaniamma: Mother Love and Matricide

Nalapat Balamaniamma's poems shun overtly political subjects. Time and again they return to the theme of mother and child, a dyad at the heart of an idealized world where natural harmony prevails. If there are times when the hope she overtly espouses seems slightly forced—'I have tried my best,' she wrote in a foreword to a 1970 edition of her poems, 'to keep my optimism undimmed...poetry as an art beneficial to humanity must make [man] know his unconquerable ever-evolving inner being, not his weakness'—more often than not, her work is molded to suit the subtle, deliberate range of her emotions, within the scope of which she is capable of great refinement.[16]

In a poem entitled "A Mother's Heart," a woman stops in the midst of her household chores and feels 'the atoms of sunshine whirl around her.' She sees her small child playing in the compound, hears again in memory the sound of the stream, the music of the wind in the leaves, and feels utterly at peace. Her feminine centrality—the child comes to clutch at her sari's rim, the bees cluster about her, ants touch her feet—achieves a perfect poise, a noncombative, unobtrusive value. In such a notion of the feminine, there is no gap between Being and Doing, between femininity and an all-encompassing universe that nurtures humankind. The poem ends with a query, gently shifting the voice back to an enlarged self, a spiritualized maternity that is self-fulfilling. In a poem entitled "Sympathy," the feminine speaker wanders down to the river with her child. She senses the grass at her ankles, the ripples of water all along her skin, the approaching fish. She feels a most physical pleasure in the sensations. The world, tender, needy, draws close to her:

> When I lit my kitchen fire the sunbeams
> Filtered in, the Kaipa creeper peeped in
> To ask for water, the dove perches on my
> Doorstep and begged for food.

As she watches her sleeping infant, the speaker realizes why this sympathy for all living creatures wells up in her:

> The soul of the world took form to become
> Your beloved child. So you are mother,
> Mother to them all.

At least on the surface of it, there is nothing in these earlier images to prepare us for violence. It was thirty-two years later, in 1966, that the poet published her complex, anguished portrayal of maternal murder and its aftermath: "The Story of the Axe." As with Sita forced to the test by fire, as with the young girls on Gandhi's Tolstoy Farm, it is female sexuality that betrays the culturally sanctioned feminine.

The sage Jamadagni, unable to bear the awareness that his young, lovely wife might in thought, if not in deed, have sexual desires from which he is exempt, orders her death. Each of his sons refuses matricide. Only Parasurama, in his perfect adherence to dharma, fulfills his father's command. In her reflections on her own poetry, Balamaniamma writes that in the poem she has tried to show 'the utter futility of strength and power based on violence.' Her point is amply borne out in the terrible remorse that strikes Parasurama, who looks back on his act of maternal murder, all his peace destroyed, a son betrayed by dharma. Yet as in all tragic thought, there is fatal necessity to this suffering, a perfection achieved at the very end. The lovely land of Kerala has risen up from the spot where Parasurama's bloody axe fell.

At the heart of the poem is Parasurama's recreation of his mother's longing as she gazes at the sexual delights of the nymphs, a memory that can do little to redeem him from the desolation of his crime, or the violent rage that led him to massacre Karthaveerya and his armies. He recounts his father's terrible jealousy, how his brothers shrink back at the paternal command to murder Renuka:

> I alone, the beloved of my father stepped forward.
> High rose my axe, Lord Shiva's gift and
> My mother's head rolled on the ground.
> There lay at our feet
> That face so gentle,
> That body which stood for humility,
> That hot blood which yearned for pleasures of the world.
> Her wide open eyes like those of a sacrificial animal
> Only held hurt and astonishment.

The poem ends with Parasurama, ages later, seated atop a sacred mountain, contemplating Kerala and its inhabitants, his countrymen, their lives 'stamped with my axe's tip,' their very beings 'tossed in the cradle of passions.'

How is this poem written by a woman relevant to our reflections on feminism and decolonization? In his overt capitulation to dharma, his tormented ability to pay the price, the fierce, masculine Parasurama portrays the destructive element into which the feminine artist must plunge in order to refine her craft. The poise, the sensuous if innocent enjoyment of Balamaniamma's maternal figures, repeat if only in negativity, as the reader contemplates the sin of Jamadagni's wife—sexual desire.

For Balamaniamma the poet, Parasurama, in obeying his father's law, violates his mother. This was a radical insight, one with massive repercussions. Quite deliberately, Balamaniamma rewrites the familiar Puranic version of the myth where the instant after she is murdered, Renuka, in keeping with her son's wish, is brought back whole, live and well through her husband's mystic powers. In the poem, the son is betrayed by dharma, the mother cannot be brought back to life, and Parasurama is left to vent his rage in more and more murderous acts.

A grotesque, yet telling episode in *Agnisakshi* comes to mind. Tethi, renamed Devi Bahen in her Gandhian incarnation, takes a young refugee from Pakistan into her ashram. She befriends the woman, renaming her Thankam. Unknown to her, this Thankam has an affair with another inmate of the ashram, a young man from the South who may well be a terrorist. He flees when the police arrive. The new Thankam, meanwhile, has been suffering from fainting fits and vomiting. When Devi Bahen goes in to look on her, she comes upon a grotesque sight:

'Thankam was seen strangling the neck of a newborn child, struggling in a pool of blood. Her eyes blazed. She gritted her teeth. There was a demonic thrust to her lips. Her expression was fierce like that of Bhadrakali who strangled the neck of the demon Darika and drank blood.'[17]

Sexual guilt consumes this second Thankam and she murders her helpless, newborn infant, symbol of the land itself. Slowly, deliberately, she strangles the child, explaining to Devi Bahen that she cannot bear to let her child live in a world of such terrible violence. She would rather take its life.

The horrific image, never fully integrated into the narrative, is crucial though to the outcaste power that Lalithambika Antherjanam seeks. A power dimly symbolized in her novel in the burning of the temple, a power masked over and forbidden by dharma, a power that the great reformer Gandhi, for all his edgy puritanism, was deeply aware of, but sometimes couldn't face.

Lalithambika Antherjanam: Outcaste Power

At the heart of Lalithambika Antherjanam's great, controversial work, *Agnisakshi*, lies the ritual displacement of women. The protagonist is first seen as a bride being led into her new household. But the gaze that is turned on her comes from a young girl, Thankam, thrust away from the marriage ceremonies for fear she might pollute the ritual. As the child of a Nair mother and Namboodiri father, the child is considered inauspicious. Her shame and rage carry over in the voice of the adult narrator in a work that deals with the repression undercutting culture and ceremony, the splintering of the iconic feminine, the dissolution of identities.

Even as the bride, Tethi, is granted entry to the inner sanctum of the house, the child, Thankam, runs away, locks herself up in a room and refuses to come out. Tethi, in turn, finds herself alone and isolated in the orthodox household into which she has married. In desperation at her married life, the new bride writes to her brother, an ardent political activist, who reads her discontent not as an isolated event, but as part of a larger political unrest rocking the country.

When her brother is imprisoned by the British and made an outcaste by his own community, Tethi bears the shame and horror of it all. She lies weeping by the toilet as the old grandmother curses her: 'Siva! Siva! Our young Namboodiris are such thoughtless people; they eat along with untouchables; they lose their proper perception; they even opt to go to jail.'

Antherjanam draws a direct connection between the ferocity that boils, unseen, within Tethi and the rising discontent in the country. The woman who must break loose is also India, which must break free of colonial domination. In each case there is pain, terror, and a massive disruption, as well as a slow and difficult progression from darkness into light.

After Tethi escapes from the illam, a photo of her appears in the local newspapers under a caption that reads, 'From darkness to light.' The narrator sees a dim image, a woman in a sari and blouse, standing on a platform. Fascinated, she reads the newspaper account of the speech made by the fiery Devaki Manampalli (as Tethi is now known):

'I do not represent any particular community, religion or society. I am the representative of the womenfolk who have been subjected to suffering for centuries. Looking at this truth which stands before you, veil discarded, you may curse or bless. But this load of sorrow which is our very own was your creation.'

But sorrow does not remain static, confining. There is a power of release, a fierce, female Shakti that all the characters in the novel must reckon with. The novel itself, with its title *Agni-sakshi*, is a direct allusion to the witness or trial by fire which Sita had to pass. Humiliated by Rama, forced by him to prove her chastity by passing through fire, Sita cried out to her mother earth, and the earth split open and swallowed her.

The young Tethi, shut up in the family home, had turned bit by bit into a skin with fire inside. 'Oh my sister-in-law! Is this you? Was your inside a volcano?' muses Thankam. But the symbolic feminine, even as it draws on the power invested in it by the culture, turns tormenting to the flesh and blood woman. There is nowhere available to the woman who has revolted. Identity slips and slides in this unstable world. Tethi must keep changing her names—she becomes Devki Manampalli, Devi Bahen, Sumitrananada the ascetic—her varied names indicative of a world so swiftly transforming that female identity is necessarily irresolute, mobile, anguished.

The struggle for decolonization has borne with it the fragile shelters of order. 'Homes were ruined, the way was cleared,' the narrator muses. But nothing is wholly clarified for the voice that must seek a new world. After national independence, there is no obvious place the freed woman can go. Old, infirm, though with a steely will, in her last incarnation as a Holy Mother, Tethi is forced to confront her own past self. But this means facing up to the sexual rage that forced her outwards, a fierce pain the political world has never quite assuaged. Stumbling on this self she has constantly fled, the heroine faces the voice that is great within her, bearing the strength of Otherness. A voice that confronts the grotesque, becomes one with it, so that the useless categories of religious observance, the powerlessness and humiliation that can come from being a colonized woman, are owned up to.

And if her femininity, refined, struck into the stern discipline of an ascetic's life, found strength by molding itself to religious rituals that had prevailed for centuries, this other voice gathers the moral courage to spell out violation, mutilation, sexual bondage, the ferocity that can lie in the hearts of mothers and daughters. Lying on the cold earth near Varanasi, just as she had lain on the damp ground by the toilet in her husband's illam, she cries out:

'O Earth! who suffers everything. What all she stores in her mind's recesses. Black serpents, hard rocks, crores and crores of human civilizations and their ruins. The voices of ages slumber there. Green surface with fire inside. Oh Sita! Mother of all human beings! You sought protection here. Please accept me also.'

What might it mean to be accepted by the mother earth? Is it a longing for flight, a woman's consciousness pitched to despair? Or is this possibly a true and final vindication? That the earth split open to receive Sita demonstrated her purity, the womb of earth drawing the daughter in after all the humiliation of an earthly life.

And pondering the novel, here, now in New York City, I think: is this the penalty paid for female desire? At what cost such purity? And my mind moves on: what bond does the body of the immigrant woman bear to the North American soil? Particularly here, in this metropolis where there is so little earth visible.

At the very end of *Manhattan Music,* the novel I have just finished writing, the protagonist stumbles into Central Park. She does not know where else to go. Perhaps if I could, I would have her buried in soil, with delicate holes for breathing, so that cast into the earth she could emerge again, whole. But since this work is not overtly surreal in intent, I have her encounter an old man who plays the saxophone. His clothes now are in rags, a stench comes out of him. Sandhya wanders on, discovers a small pond, sits on a bare rock and sees her own face, quivering in the water. The recognition startles her. She is free then, to move on, into the city, quickly. The last word of the sentence, that adverb, is something I had stored in my head, for years and years after I first finished reading D. H. Lawrence's *Sons and Lovers* in Nottingham, that grey midlands city where the grass burns with sunlight in winter, where slag heaps still lie open to the sky.

What is near to us? What is close at hand? The voice that is other grows great. It bursts through the body. It sings. The world that Lalithambika Antherjanam wrote from is not far from me. I bear it within. It becomes part of the memory I need for knowledge of this new world, part of a migrant music.

Theater of Sense

What follows is an imaginary dialogue with a Kathakali dancer who leaps through the open window, into my room in Manhattan.

Kathakali, the traditional dance drama of Kerala, in South India, is danced by men. Elaborate costumes and face paintings are required for the dance. Men play the parts of women, with both male and female characters drawn from ancient mythology.

This male dancer plays the part of Draupadi, wife to the five Pandavas, heroine of the Mahabharata, exiled from her homeland.

Only half of his face is painted. Did haste consume him, the febrile passage westwards? Or was it sheer necessity, lack of funds, that sort of thing? Or then again, was this a deliberate act, a secret signal?

I.

He approaches me, a man with long nails, glittering red. His eyes are rimmed with kohl. A parrot hops up and down on his shoulder.

He whispers to me in Malayalam, 'va kochu, va.'

I open my hands and he sets an instrument in them, a long-limbed thing, made of a painted gourd.

So many strings, I weep to see them tangled in my fingers. The sound is that of a goat readied for sacrifice, braying in a desert land I'll never see again. When I wake, all I have is the heaviness in my hands.

He comes again the next night, with him another, a man, so slender, dressed as a woman in the manner of the Kathakali dancers. She is Draupadi, hair grown wild with exile. They dance across my room, pointing, wordlessly. When I wake up objects leap into my hands, a bit of cardboard, a broken clay bowl, long metal wires on the broken sill.

With them I try to forge an instrument, a crude thing. I do not know what music will come of it, but it's all I have to set the dancers athrob, to make up a migrant music.

II.

When next I see her, she asks me questions, the man/woman Draupadi who came dancing into my room. Questions of sense and nonsense. Out of her undifferentiated world, where history as I have known it holds little sway, comes the voice. A febrile ventriloquism. Her voice comes to me in the darkness of dream, that first theater of sense, where the 'metaphysic of gesture'* is clarified.

Her ankles decked with bells, swathed in her silks, she is ready for Kathakali, ancient dance drama of Kerala. One side of her face is exquisitely painted, the layers of vegetable-based dyes, the white and the red, overlaying each other in intricate balances. The other half is bare. How odd she looks. The dull brown of the skin peeps through, the fragile lips, nude, shimmering as the petals of a waterlily might at twilight, bled of coloration.

So she stands, each part of her face mocking the other, a profane predicament that draws me closer. She seems to be sweating a little. Perhaps it is hot in my room.

Why should she come, asking these questions? What does she want of me? She is earnest though, stooped a little like a studious undergraduate, her chin propped on a wrist, delicate, bird-like.

---

* Note: I borrow the phrase 'metaphysic of gesture' from Antonin Artaud, "On the Balinese Theatre," in *The Theater and its Double.*

She speaks at first in English, with some difficulty, switching to Malayalam as the emotion catches hold of her:

Draupadi: So what brought you here?

Meena Alexander: Here?

D: You know what I mean, America.

MA: I'm not sure. Perhaps I came to remember my life.

D: You're mad!

At this she shakes her head a little, does a dance. My foot soles throb as I watch her. From the middle distance comes music, an unseen voice which sings of Draupadi's exile.

MA: Perhaps I came to make it all up. Name things afresh, here and there. Except the past caught me by the throat. I feel I am noosed in a lasso, a figure of eight. Does that make sense?

Let me begin again: I came here, Draupadi, to live and write. To face these mountains, the setting sun. To bristle with life, as a porcupine might.

This brown skin, what does it do to me? I don't paint it all up as you do. It's naked and they take me for many things—Trinidadian, Guyanan, Mexican even. Sometimes Indian. I am always marked in that way.

How can I remember, you're wondering? What can I remember? Everything that rushes in, settles in me, becomes the past. I write this as I can, naming things afresh.

D: You never think of going back? (How quiet her voice is.)

MA: Of course I do, but I'm here. The world comes to me here. India, America: all these are names for worlds we live in. We are in the middle, you and I. Where the breath of heaven blows down on us, cool or biting hot, we make our home. And sometimes it's all stripped away, the names, places, and only the localities survive. The borderlands we make for ourselves, digging up earth with our hands. And our bodies, too, are stripped, to get to the core of naming.

D: Ayo, Ayo. Kalyanathine po!

She starts leaping up and down at this, jangling her bells. What have I done to amuse her? She pretends to loosen the top of her blouse. Then starts tensing her toes to dance. She moves her right hand out in the mark of the bee approaching a lotus flower, gestures with the other hand so I might go on speaking. What does she want of me? That I might be her double, babbling while she dances, mocking me?

MA: Listen, Draupadi, I went to England recently. I was invited to give some readings. I read poems and bits of my autobiography in a prison. The room was crowded with men. Fifty people in a small library in HMP Stocken. And do you know what happened right after I finished reading? (She is staring out of the window now, but I feel she is listening to me.) One of the men stood up, a tall, thin man.

D: Indian?

MA: No, a white man.

D: But aren't there Indians in prison there?

MA: Of course there are. Don't be foolish. But this was a white man, in a pinstriped shirt, regulation wear for prisoners. They wear that with jeans or dark sweat suits. A thin man with sharp eyes. His question took my breath away.

D: So?

MA: What do you mean, so?

D: I mean what did he ask?

MA: 'What effect has colonialism had on your work?'

D: What's that supposed to mean?

MA: He meant the British coming to India, ruling it for 250 years and more. Teaching us English.

D: But we drove them out. Did Gandhi live in vain?

MA: Of course not, but there's an aftermath, remember? (I said this as gently as I could.) The man was asking me about what comes after colonialism. The shock waves we carry in our bodies. Arriving in America has clarified that. Hitting land. Hitting this continent Christopher Columbus thought was India. Though of course, six years after Columbus, in 1498, Vasco da Gama landed in Kozikodhe.

D: Ah! (She lets out a sigh of relief hearing the name of the town where she was born.) There are no good dancing schools there, though. Do you know that? I had to go far away, to Kochi, to train. (She pauses.)

What did you say to that Englishman?

MA: I think he was Irish. At least he said so, and why would he make up something like that. The first I heard of prisons, I told him, was from my grandparents on my mother's side, who were followers of Gandhi. For several years they were in constant fear of imprisonment by the British.

Of course colonialism has had an effect. The language I use, it has an edge for me, a subtle violence, I embrace. Sometimes I feel it is tearing me apart. Or am I tearing it?

D: (Hurriedly.) I feel that with the singer for my dances. In a way, he sets the rhythm. Or thinks he is supposed to.

MA: Can't blame it all on colonialism! (We both laugh a little nervously.) The education I received, what has it made of me? It's all crept inside me, another body doubled up in mine.

Hey, Draupadi, why do you keep your face like that, half-painted, half-nude? (She turns away from me, her wrists trembling; she refuses to answer.) You're divided, too, aren't you? Well, in any case, it's not like clothing you can tear off, is it? More like skin.

Gandhi made a mass of mill-woven clothing and burnt it to high heaven. Part of his satyagraha, the way of truth. The same man who stepped off the boat in England dressed in white flannels and top hat. Took French lessons, dancing lessons. He felt all those were things he had to do to live properly. Of course, it was before he saw through British power. Saw through to the other side. Then his body became an instrument, he built up his own aesthetic.

D: Was he satisfied?

MA: Gandhi?

D: No, the prisoner at HMP Stocken, with what you said.

MA: I guess. Though I did admit it was an awfully hard question. A bit like asking: 'What effect has God had on your work?'

D: (She keeps a deadpan expression. I wonder if she's offended.) So what of America?

MA: What of America?

D: How does it all work here? How does your music change?

MA: You know I'm not a musician.

D: Your words, then, and the shadow of your words. That difficult harmony. (She tapped her long nails impatiently at the windowsill.) You see even my nails leave shadows. They move, keep moving.

MA: It's all accidental, raw, brutal here.

D: Silly!

MA: No, really, I have no tradition here. What can I draw on?

D: (She points around the room, then out the window at the bare blue bowl of the sky.) It's one world, isn't it?

MA: Is it?

D: You tell me. I'm not going to give you all the answers.

MA: I feel I'm on thin ground, ready to fall through.

D: Really?

MA: Henry David Thoreau, that New England guy Gandhi loved to read. He has a bit in his pond book about standing at the edge, looking at the ice then thinking, if I cut through that, jump through that, I'll end up in India. Right through the earth, onto the other side.

D: But that wasn't what I was asking.

MA: How did you get to be so harsh?

D: It's my dance discipline. All those years, my dear! (She lifts up her sari, pats her calf muscles.) I was asking how all that colonialism stuff you spoke of to that chap in prison works for you in America.

MA: I must interrupt you. I gave a reading at a college in Maine.

D: Where's that? Tamil Nadu?

MA: No, in America. A cold place, lots of ice and snow and woods, right by a brilliant blue sea. You can see whales there. I gave a reading in a huge hall, Muskie Auditorium, on the college campus. The place was packed. Before I began, one of the student organizers pulled me aside.

'Listen,' she whispered, 'there's a little problem.'

'What's that?'

'Well, the student newspaper that has advertised your reading.'

'Yes?'

'It has a picture of you in a sari, but the caption under it says, 'Meena Alexander, Native-American poet reads today.'

'Native American?'

'Yes. We wrote Indian, of course. And you are the first Asian Indian to read here. But the editor, wanting to be politically correct, crossed it out, and put Native American instead.'

D: So what did you do?

MA: What could I do? Before reading poems, I spoke of the mix-up, saying I was deeply honored to be considered a Native American, but I was not. Then I spoke of the white man's naming pattern, Columbus, Vasco da Gama, and the dream of India.

Even when he was hauled off, mad and raving, Columbus never admitted he hadn't found India.

D: Why would he, especially when he'd gone crazy?

MA: What can I say, Draupadi? And for all of us Asian Indians here, it's still too soon to tell how things will crystallize. But I do sense it's a struggle for a new form of life.

We need to carry over a lot, invent our place so we don't slip and slide on thin ice with nowhere to be. Fall through into a hole and land up in ether. Nowhere!

D: Here am I!

She murmured this and started dancing in the room, the long, elaborate dance of her exile, her eyes darting, her ankles hopping and flying, the long tresses coming loose in the heat of our makeshift theater.

III.

It was when I saw her for the last time that I tried to explain something else to Draupadi. I had just been to see the Jacob Lawrence retrospective at the Museum of Modern Art. I told

Draupadi that I felt I was like the girl in Jacob Lawrence's image in the *Migration Series. No. #33.* The one with the caption:

'People who had not yet come North received letters from their relatives telling them of the better conditions that existed in the North.'

Then I started to speak of the black girl, her thin shoulders hunched on the green-hooded bed, eyes buried in her face as the other, her sister surely, lies down to concentrate better, hair spread out, body massed on the bed, shielded by green covers, reading aloud the letter.

'It's a flimsy blue letter, like those air letters that come from India. Only this is from Chicago or New York.' I tell Draupadi. And she listens, head cocked out of the window, as I muse on absence, longing, the harshness of brown walls marked with thick yellow lines. Then I ponder what it might have cost the painter to buy those paints during the Depression.

She turns on me suddenly: 'But you're the one who's gone North, the one who might have sent the letter.'

'I thought you weren't listening!'

She laughs in my face. But then presses her point.

'It isn't really you, is it?'

I suddenly feel the blood rush to my face. Slowly, as if I were the singer of the songs she dances to, I intone my speech, slipping into the rhythms of Malayalam:

'I am the sister who went away and the sister who stayed behind.

The writer of the letter and the reader, too. The distance that cuts and curves this curtainless theater of accidents, composes my soul.'

As I speak, I see her listen silently, dancer, muse, dark, divided double.

Together we mark the quick step of marginality.

Aftermath: Title Search

I was speaking on the phone to a friend. The conversation turned to what I was writing.

'Do you have a title?' she asked.

'I think I've figured it out.' I took my time saying it: *The Shock of Arrival*. I felt the words turn over on my tongue as if I had thought of the phrase for the first time.

'I like that,' she mused. Her voice was soft.

In the silence, I felt the blood rush to my head. She of all people would surely know, and there I was, only then realizing where the title came from.

'It's like an explosion in my head,' I mumbled to her. 'You know I hadn't thought of it till this very moment. I guess it was buried in me, where it comes from.'

I stopped, embarrassed at my own intensity, and turned the conversation to something else.

A whole day later, on the bus—somehow the fact of the moving vehicle comforted me, the slow resolute speed, the heaviness of the metal body—I opened V.S. Naipaul's *Enigma of Arrival*.

There it was, the description of the Chirico image that had so moved him: the ship, the wharf, the traveler left behind, and then the unselving, the nightmare that ended with an explosion in the head that the author never really absorbed into his narrative.

'The shock of arrival!' I murmured the words to myself.

Why had I kept it to myself, buried the words under the skin of my mind—or not the words, really, but their provenance?

What was the 'damage' Naipaul alluded to, his person-hood buried under the 'writing personality'? I had been more open, at least with myself, about the connection with Walter Benjamin, the 'shock' of memory he reveals, the clarity, the illumination that rises up at a moment of danger. But almost as if I was ashamed of it, I had forgotten this other, murkier bond, closer to home.

Well Jumped Women

In 1995, I was in England writing and giving readings at the invitation of the Arts Council. One of the readings was in a library in Leicester. The audience was not made up of the usual literary types and college students. They were older Indian women, migrants from East Africa. Many of them had no memories of India. It was the landscape of Africa that they remembered, that moved them.

The plan was for me to read from my work—poems, prose pieces, whatever I chose. The group's translator would render my words in Gujurati. Later I would answer questions. This had worked well for an earlier group I had met, so I was not apprehensive.

The translator, a substitute as it turned out, stepped forward briskly. A middle-aged Indian man, dressed in a shiny three-piece suit, he pointed to the circle of women, seated and waiting.

After the Arts Council organizer left the room, he turned to me. 'Literature, eh?' he asked, his voice throaty. 'What use is it?'

'Look at those women. Illiterate all of them. Now, if you had come to help them read the gas meter or pay their medical bills, that would have been something.'

He stood on the balls of his feet, a little man, cocky, upright. 'What use, eh?' He stopped suddenly. One of the women approached us, and offered me a cup a tea.

The man looked at me.

'No, they have to pay a little something for the tea, but not you.' He pushed a chair forward.

I sat next to him in the half circle. The sunlight was like pale water, falling through a high window. My mind slipped to my first time in England, in the fall of 1969. I had just arrived from Sudan, a young woman of eighteen years. With my departure for England, my family were returning to India. We had left Khartoum forever. And there I was in England, all alone. I missed my mother's delicate brown hands, her face; my father's erect carriage, the sense of certitude he had about things. How could I even start to piece the world together, when the trees were unfamiliar and instead of the sharp blue desert skies, I had this pale wash of gray flooding over me?

They were looking at me, waiting for me to begin. The translator adjusted his tie, stared straight ahead, cleared his throat. I was nervous, and felt my voice fall a little as I started to read the poem "Blood Line."

'Poetry!' He shot out the word as if puzzled.

Surely, I thought, he had known a poet was coming. Or perhaps no one had warned him. Very quickly, for I wanted the poem to work for the listening women, I launched into my broken Hindi, hoping that it would carry the burden. It was a simple poem, really, addressed to my daughter when she was one year old. It poured back into me: the little one waved and for the very first time, turned quite simply on her short plump legs, and walked away from me. The lines ran:

When wild deer
track the mud
for buried roots

I'll grip my blouse
and loosen it
I'll show her how
my throat can hang
a woman's weight.

I made a prose rendering in English, spoke about women's lives. We broke into conversation then, the women and I, about children, mothers, shopping, bhajans, the cold of Leicester. Our translator was displeased. 'Go on, on' he commanded.

'I'll do prose next,' I volunteered, and before he could stop me, I launched into a little tale. I spoke of how as a child I had spent summer months in my grandparental home in coastal Kerala, a place of so much water, so many wells, in sharp contrast to the austerities of sky and sand in Khartoum.

One of the women spoke of the pleasure of drawing water from a well, how hot it was 'there', and the lines between the remembered worlds of Africa and India started to blur. I could see that the translator was not enjoying himself. He stirred in his chair, cleared his throat, tugged at his red necktie. But I had a tale to tell.

'When I was a small child, I was told not to go near the well. Naturally, you might think, this is just the right advice to give a child. After all, there's always the danger of toppling in. But the more I was told to stay away, the more the idea of the well fascinated me. I knew there was cool water at the base and I longed to stand on tiptoe and look in. And sometimes I did, within the safe circle of my ayah's arms.

'But I heard other things as I turned seven, then eight. So-and-so's daughter has fallen into the well. And of course, she was pregnant.

'I was haunted by the thought of a pregnant woman in the well, mother and unborn child floating together. No one had pushed them in, nor had they jumped. Just fell in—that's what I understood. Ever so furtively, I would inch toward the well and try to see her face—the face of the fallen woman. But there in the depths, sixty feet down, slipping, blurring, all I could see were my eyes, dark and open, gazing up.'

I stopped for breath. The women were listening hard. Someone spoke in a mixture of Hindi and English about the high rate of suicide among Indian women in England. I listened. But there was more to tell.

'Years later,' I began again, 'when I started to write a book about my life, that image haunted me—of women fearful, shamed out of their lives, jumping into wells. I wound my way round and around. Suddenly the thought came: why not have them jump over the wells, instead of jumping into them? Then came the phrase with its own subdued music: *well jumped women.* So with that phrase humming in my ears I made a short prose piece about a Kerala house and countless women, jumping over wells. I put that fragment into a chapter called "Khartoum Journal."'

I picked up my book and started reading:

A voice comes to me out of mist and desert rain, out of well water and water in a blackened cooking pot where I looked in and saw my face: "You come from a long line of well-jumped women."

Women come to me, countless women, some older, some younger: sixty-year-olds, hair bleached by time, stretched back tight over the skull, knotted at the nape; twenty-year-olds, their sweet hair hovering over the mouth, black hair blown back over the mouth in monsoon winds; four-year-old children playing hopscotch, then swooped above ground on a wooden swing, hair brushing the branches of the love apple tree; babies too, plump, cheeks marked with beauty spots to keep away the evil eye, soft mouths dribbling milk.

And in the courtyard of a Kerala house I see worlds filled with women, women riding elephants, women like Princess Chitrangada with swords at their hips, bodies covered in rough jute—and who can see the softness of cotton underneath, stained with menstrual blood? I see women, saris swept up shamelessly, high above the ankles, high above the knees, women well-jumping: jumping over wells.

For a few seconds there was quiet and then a swarm of questions. 'I understand,' said one woman, 'but why, why?' 'Did it happen often?' asked another. 'Of course it happens all the time,' said a third, her voice rising, 'and sometimes it's fire.'

The translator snapped to attention, cleared his throat, stood very straight, staring at me.

'So?' he said, sharply, almost waiting for me to respond. Then he went on, slow, resolute: 'I refuse to translate that.'

Anger rose in me. I tried to control my voice. One word would be enough, surely.

'Why?'

His tones were very clear: 'Madam, those women *should* jump into the well.'

I could sense the shock in the room. I faced him squarely, inchoately musing until some sense broke free; I breathed deep, looked at the small man looming over me, my mind skirmishing with his rage. I did not come from so far away, nor did the other women, I thought, to quarrel with the translator. He believes what he says, I thought to myself, silently.

But then I snapped back, ready to battle: 'That's ridiculous.'

'Better you should tell us about Kerala,' the man responded. 'Yes, much better. Palm trees, back waters. I run a travel agency, you know that?'

And he pressed a business card into my palm. *That* is what I am writing against, I thought, my palm with the business card, burning. Later I felt so frail, like paper stretched over the mouth of a well. I thought of a room with a high window, the weak sun pouring through, the women gathered there, the translator's abrupt refusal. And I pondered what my tale of jumping over wells might have meant to the women gathered in the room, and what else might have passed through all our minds in that brief, disturbing space.

Notes

The Shock of Arrival

1. *Vivekachudamani of Sri Sankaracharya,* trans. Swami Madhavanada (Calcutta: Advaita Ashram, 1974). #39: 'Lord…do thou sprinkle me who am tormented by worldly afflictions as by the tongues of a forest-fire.' #41: 'As he speaks thus, tormented by the afflictions of the world—which is like a forest on fire…'

2. These and other statements by the artists formed part of the exhibit and were displayed on the walls next to the artwork. Also see exhibit catalog: *Asia\America: Identities in Contemporary Asian-American Art* (New York: Asia Society Galleries/The New Press, 1994).

3. Ralph Waldo Emerson, "Self Reliance," in *Selected Works of Ralph Waldo Emerson,* William H. Gilman, ed. (New York: New American Library, 1965), 268.

4. Michel Foucault, *Discipline and Punish: The Birth of the Prison* (New York: Pantheon, 1977), 30.

5. Benjamin Franklin, "Observations Concerning the Increase of Mankind," in *The Papers of Benjamin Franklin,* ed. Leonard W. Labaree, vol. 4 (New Haven: Yale University Press, 1959), 234.

6. Frantz Fanon, *The Wretched of the Earth* (Harmondsworth: Penguin, 1968), 61.

Skin with Fire Inside

1. H. S. L. Polak, H. N. Brailsford, and Lord Pethick-Lawrence, *Mahatma Gandhi,* foreword and appreciation by H. E.

Sarojini Naidu, Governor of the United Provinces (London: Odhams Press, 1949), 7.

2. Eleanor Morton, *Women Behind the Mahatma Gandhi* (London: Max Reinhardt, 1954), 158.

3. Sarojini Naidu, *The Golden Threshold*, intro. Arthur Symons (London: William Heinemann, 1909), 9, 11, 16, 17.

4. Sarojini Naidu, *The Sceptered Flute; Songs of India: The Collected Poems of Sarojini Naidu* (New York: Dodd, Mead, 1928), 53.

5. Arthur Symons, *Silhouettes*, 2nd ed. (London: Leonard Smithers, 1896), 13 ("Morbidezza"). "Maquillage" is included in *Poetry of the Nineties*, ed. R. K. R. Thornton (Harmondsworth: Penguin, 1970), 44-45.

6. See Padmini Sengupta, *Sarojini Naidu: A Biography* (Bombay: Asia Publishing House, 1966), 48-49.

7. Quoted in Srinivasa Iyengar, *Indian Writing in English*, 2nd ed. (New York: Asia Publishing House, 1973), 44.

8. Sarojini Naidu, *Speeches and Writings* (Madras: Natesan, 1918), 16.

9. *Speeches*, 92.

10. Pattabhi Sitaramayya, ed., *The History of the Indian National Congress, Vol. 1: 1885-1935* (Bombay: Padma Publications, 1946), 290—for the message published by the president-elect, October 1925.

11. A. M. Zaidi and S. G. Zaidi, eds., *The Encyclopedia of the Indian National Congress, Vol. 9: 1925-1929* (New Delhi: S. Chand, 1980), 30-31.

12. See Ketu Katrak, "Indian Nationalism, Gandhian 'Satyagraha' and Representations of Female Sexuality," in *Nationalisms and Sexualities*, eds. Andrew Parker, Mary Russo, Doris Sommer, and Patricia Yaeger (New York: Routledge, 1992) for an insightful exploration of the complexities of domestic and political spheres in which women of the Gandhian era were caught.

13. Madhu Kishwar, *Gandhi and Women* (Delhi: Manushi Prakashan, 1986), 3, 19, 22. I am indebted to Madhu Kishwar's analysis of Gandhi's views on femininity and nonviolence. Also relevant are Ashis Nandy's views on how gender entered into

British colonial discourse, with Indian men seen by the colonizers as effeminate—a stance that Gandhi was able to reformulate for his own nationalist purposes. See Ashis Nandy, "The Psychology of Colonialism," in *The Intimate Enemy: Loss and Recovery of Self Under Colonialism* (Delhi: Oxford University Press, 1983), 48-55.

14. M. K. Gandhi, "Satyagraha in South Africa," *The Selected Works of Mahatma Gandhi*, ed. Shriman Narayan, vol. 3 (Ahmedabad: Navjivan Trust, 1968), 333.

15. M. K. Gandhi, *An Autobiography, or the Story of my Experiments with Truth: Selected Works*, vol. 1. See Chapter 9, "My Father's Death and My Double Shame."

16. Nalapat Balamaniamma, *Thirty Poems* (Madras: Orient Longman, 1970), from the Foreword.

17. Lalithambika Antherjanam, *Agnisakshi*, trans. Vasanthi Sankaranarayanan (Trichur: Kerala Sahitya Akademi, 1980), 103.

Acknowledgements

I wish to acknowledge the publishers of the journals and books where the following poems and prose pieces first appeared:

Poetry

These poems first appeared in my published volumes of poetry. "House of a Thousand Doors," "Hotel Alexandria," "Poem by the Wellside," "Looking through Well Water," "Great Brown River," "Sidi Syed's Architecture," and "'A garden inclosed is my sister, my spouse...'" (under the title, "A Note on the Writer Balamaniamma") were published in *House of a Thousand Doors* (Washington, DC: Three Continents Press, 1988).

"Her Mother's Words" was first published in *I Root My Name* (Calcutta: United Writers, 1977).

"After the First House" and "The Travellers" were published in *The Storm: A Poem in Five Parts* (New York: Red Dust, 1989).

"Kochi Harbor," "Aunt Chinna," "Alphabet of Flesh," "Threshold Song," and "Glimpsed in Indigo" were published in *Night-Scene, the Garden* (New York: Red Dust, 1989).

"Art of Pariahs," "Passion," "Skin Song," "Ashtamudi Lake," "Estrangement Becomes the Mark of the Eagle," "For Safdar Hashmi," "Moloyashree," "Paper Filled with Light," and "San Andreas Fault" were published in *River and Bridge* (New Delhi: Rupa, 1995; Toronto: TSAR Press, 1996). "Paper Filled with Light" was first published in *Grand Street* #39 (1991).

Prose

In somewhat different form, "Language and Shame: Reflections on my Life in Letters," was first published in *IKON*, Winter 1991.

The note to "Skin Song" was published in *Critical Survey* (UK), vol. 4, no. 2 (1992). Part of "Translating Violence" first appeared as a foreword to the anthology *Blood into Ink: South Asian and Middle Eastern Women Write War*, eds. Miriam Cooke and Roshni-Rustomji-Kerns (Boulder: Westview Press, 1994).

"Piecemeal Shelters" was first presented at the colloquium "The Literature of Displacement: the Writer and the South Asian Diaspora," November 23, 1991, University of Pennsylvania. It was published in *Public Culture*, volume 5 (1993): 621-625, © 1993 by the University of Chicago.

Part of the prose in "Tangled Roots" was published as a section of "The Poem's Second Life: Writing and Self-Identity," in *Toronto South Asian Review*, vol. 6, no. 2 (1987-88): 77-85. "Performing the Word" based on a statement read at the Dag Hammarskjold Plaza, United Nations, New York as part of the PEN "Freedom to Write" meeting, March 15, 1989, was first published in *Toronto South Asian Review*, vol. 8, no.3 (1990): 28-33.

"New World Aria" was published in *Re-Visioning Feminism Around the World*. (New York: Feminist Press, 1995)

"That Other Body" was published in *The Journal of South Asian Writing*, special issue on women immigrant writers, vol. 21, no.1 (1986)

"No Nation Woman" was published in the anthology *Her Mother's Ashes*, ed. Nurjehan Aziz (Toronto: TSAR Press, 1994).

"A Durable Past" is based in part on remarks made at the Asian-American Arts Alliance Conference "Defining Our Cultures, Defining Ourselves," June 8, 1991, Hunter College, subsequently published as "Is There an Asian American Aesthetic?" in *Art Spiral* (Winter 1991).

"The Shock of Arrival: Body, Memory, Desire in Asian-American Art" was first presented as the keynote address to the

"Symposium on Asian-American Art," Teachers' College, Columbia University, April 22, 1994. It was subsequently published in *Women and Performance*, double issue on "New Hybrid Identities," vol. 7, no. 2/vol. 8, no. 1 (1995): 14-15, 311-324.

"Making Up Memory" first took shape as remarks at a panel presentation, "Writers in the City," February 9, 1994, Fordham University at Lincoln Center. These thoughts were elaborated at the conference "Strategizing Cultures: An Asian American Dialogue on Humanities and the Arts," University of California at Los Angeles, April 29-30, 1994. The essay was published in *Women and Performance*, double issue on "New Hybrid Identities," vol. 7, no. 2/vol. 8, no. 1 (1995): 14-15, 29-37.

An earlier version of "In Search of Sarojini Naidu" was published in *Economic and Political Weekly* under the title "Sarojini Naidu: Romanticism and Resistance," special number, *Review of Women's Studies*, vol. 20, no. 43 (1985). Reprinted in *Ariel: A Review of International English Literature* (Calgary), vol. 17, no. 4, (1986): 49-61. A somewhat different version of "Fracturing the Iconic Feminine" was presented under the title "Ritual Displacement and Virile Maternity: Feminism and Decolonization in Indian Women Writers," as the Frances Wayland Collegium Lecture, October 14, 1987, Brown University. It was published in *Economic and Political Weekly* (India), February 18, 1989 vol. 24, no. 7, and in *The Journal of Commonwealth Literature* (London).

Index

"The Story of the Axe" (Balama-
niamma), 186-88
Suicide, 176, 177, 205-7
Sun, May, 153-54
"Suttee" (Naidu), 176, 177
Symons, Arthur, 5, 175, 176
"Sympathy" (Balamaniamma),
186

T

Tamil language, 4
"Tangled Roots" (Alexander), 35-
39
"The Temple" (Naidu), 180, 181
"That Other Body" (Alexander),
111
Tolstoy Farm (Gandhi), 81-82,
183-85, 186
Traditionalism: and femininity, 3,
4-5, 7, 67-70, 142, 169-71, 173,
174, 175-76, 185-88, 189-91; hierarchy, 3, 7, 12, 169-71; household order, 3; and language, 3,
4-5, 12, 39; and nationalism, 1, 7,
39; public order, 3; and
women's clothing, 68-69, 70, 78,
81. See also Colonialism; Immigrants; Postcolonialism
"The Travellers" (Alexander), 104-
10
"Two Faces, One Woman" (Samara), 85

U

United States: immigrant artists
in, 152-64; immigrants passing
in, 65-66, 68; and memory, 156-
57; multiculturalism in, 83, 157-
58. See also Immigrants
Unnamable (Beckett), 63

V

Violence: of English language, 4,
5; and female writing, 4, 5, 6, 7,
81, 84-87, 128, 130-32, 162-63;
Persian Gulf War, 78, 163; and
postcolonialism, 6, 81, 162-63;
and racism, 7, 64-65, 68, 78, 158;
and suicide, 176, 177, 205-7

W

"White Horseman Blues" (Alexander), 122-25
Whitman, Walt, 122, 129
Women: as artists, 155-56; and
childbirth, 15-26, 177-78, 183-85,
205-7; and clitoridectomy, 81;
and feminism, 81-84, 177-79,
182-85; and grandmother figures, 28, 35-48; and Manavi
(New Jersey), 83; and patriarchy, 82-83, 155, 169-71; and
Sakhi (New York), 83; and
shame, 10-12, 16, 205-7; and suicide, 176, 177, 205-7; traditional
clothing of, 68-69, 70, 78, 81; and
traditional femininity, 3, 4-5, 7,

67-70, 142, 169-71, 173, 174, 175-76, 185-88, 189-91; and violence, 4, 5, 6, 7, 81, 84-87, 128, 130-32, 162-63. *See also* Female writing; Immigrants

Y

Yong Soon Min, 160